The

In-Between

Church:

Navigating Size
Transitions in
Congregations

ALICE MANN

An Alban Institute Publication

Library of Congress Catalog Card Number 98-73670
ISBN 1-56699-207-9

CONTENTS

Foreword   vii
Richard F. Holloway

Introduction   ix

Chapter 1. What Is a Size Transition?   1
    Weighing the Giant Fly   1
    The Ramp and the Stairs   3
    No Room at the Inn—or Too Much?   6
    Living in the Gap   8
    Biblical Reflection   9
    Application Exercise   10

Chapter 2. Are We Facing a Size Transition?   11
    Glass Ceiling   11
    The Plateau Zone   12
    Seeing the Invisible   13
    God Is in the Details   14
    Biblical Reflection   15
    Application Exercise   15

Chapter 3. What Happens between Sizes?   19
    Fault Lines   19
    Organism versus Organization   20
    Group-Centered versus Pastor-Centered   21
    Six Transitions   23
    The Double-Minded Church   28

Biblical Reflection   29
Application Exercise   29

Chapter 4. Should We Be Growing?   30
Opening Up the Conversation   30
The Movement from "I" to "We"   32
God Outside the Box   33
Listening to the Other   33
So . . . Should We Be Growing?   34
Biblical Reflection   36
Application Exercise   36

Chapter 5. Why Make the Sacrifice?   38
Resolving Internal Tensions   38
War and Pestilence   39
Mission Strategy   40
Spiritual Growth   41
A Life Poured Out   43
Biblical Reflection   44
Application Exercise   44

Chapter 6. Should We Add a New Worship Service?   46
A Key Decision   46
Why Try Something Different?   47
What Is a "Somewhat Different" Style?   48
A Look at the Costs   49
Critical Mass   51
Biblical Reflection   52
Application Exercise   52

Chapter 7. Should We Add Staff?   54
Staffing Debates at St. Peter's   54
Staffing for Growth   57
Typical Patterns   58
Funding New Staff   59
Biblical Reflection   60
Application Exercise   60

Chapter 8. What Will It Take to Make the Change?   62
   Adaptive Work   62
   A Holding Environment   64
   Spiritual and Institutional Urgency   65
   Powerful Partnership between Clergy and Lay Leaders   67
   Tolerance for Unhappiness   68
   Purpose and Plan   70
   Biblical Reflection   74
   Application Exercise   75

**Appendix A. How to Minister Effectively in Family, Pastoral,
   Program, and Corporate Size Churches**   77
   Roy Oswald

**Appendix B. Demographic Profiles: How Do Congregations
   Get Their Money's Worth?**   92
   Alice Mann

Notes   99

Bibliography   105

Readers may be puzzled at the phenomenon of a Scottish bishop writing a foreword to a book by an American Episcopal priest on how to navigate the complexities of size transitions, so I offer a word of explanation and introduction.

The 1988 Lambeth Conference called upon the provinces of the Anglican Communion to inaugurate a decade of evangelism and thereby precipitated a crisis for many of the bishops. My own dilemma was probably characteristic. I describe myself as a "liberal Catholic," one of the many subspecies within Anglican zoology. Historically, we have rarely been explicitly evangelistic in our missionary approach, tending instead to the magnetic model of church growth: doing our liturgy and our Christian living in a way that exerts a powerful gravitational pull on people, who are drawn by the beauty of what they see.

After Lambeth '88 it was quite obvious to me that our communion could no longer rely solely on the magnetic model of evangelism if it was to survive, let alone flourish. But most of the models of active evangelism came from within the evangelical tradition, and the methods they espoused were usually based on an understanding of the Christian message with which I was not theologically comfortable. When I tried to adapt methods evolved by evangelical Christians to the more Catholic ethos of the Scottish Episcopal Church, I encountered little success and not a little opposition. And that's when I met Alice Mann.

I was invited by the Episcopal Diocese of Arkansas to act as chaplain at one of its conferences on parish evangelism. Mann was the consultant at the conference, and she combined a passion for church growth and a skill in the methodologies that can deliver it with a theological approach and personal style that was sympathetic to our ethos. We soon appointed her as a consultant to the Scottish Episcopal Church. As a result of Mann's work with us, we have come to recognize the vexing phenomenon of "the size plateau," in which a congregation is stuck in a behavioral syndrome that makes its life and work hard to develop. Mann likened this experience to living with a turbulent adolescent, and she knows we need strategy as well as insight if we are to use the experience creatively. The fundamental insight required is an honest acknowledgment of what is happening.

Mann's gift for using every crisis as an opportunity for the practice of faith is well expressed in this little book. It is rich with organizational insight, but its theological approach is what will make it a particularly useful primer for congregations enduring the turbulence of size transitions. One of its truly incarnational insights is the importance of applying organizational theory to the life of the Church: we must understand the human nature of structures that express the Spirit. The book convincingly demonstrates that understanding institutional life can help us discern the unconscious forces that often drive the life of the church. Mann calls us to a process of self-examination that can be entertaining as well as illuminating.

In Scotland, give or take a cultural nuance or two, we'll soon be working with this book, so it gives me great pleasure to commend it to readers everywhere.

> The Most Reverend Richard F. Holloway
> Bishop of Edinburgh, Primus
> Scottish Episcopal Church

INTRODUCTION

When I was ordained 24 years ago, I had barely thought about the meaning of a congregation's size. To me, a "big church" mostly meant a cathedral-type building. Tiny, family-size congregations were also outside my comprehension. I had grown up somewhere in the middle.

My childhood parish, once a country church, found itself surrounded by the suburban explosion of the 1950s. I was in the first class of children to attend the brand-new school (still under construction for my whole elementary education) instead of the two-room building behind the church. I remember what big news it was when, for the first time, a young priest was assigned to assist Father Daly. By the time I left college, that church had far outgrown its century-old stone building, even with multiple service times, and had spawned a brand-new congregation on the other side of town. Somehow, with little theory and no consultants, that church figured out how to change size in response to its environment.

While some congregations today may still make sound, intuitive judgments about scaling up (or scaling down) in response to their environment, most church leaders find these issues daunting. I hope that the following chapters will clear away some of the fog around questions of changing size, and help you discern the leading of God for your congregation.

While the book should be useful to the individual reader, it is meant to be the sort of volume that pastors and lay leaders can pass around to each other or read in the context of a study group. Each chapter ends with a section entitled Biblical Reflection and one called Application Exercise. I hope you will not skip over the passages and questions provided. They are integral to the process of discernment.

CHAPTER 1

What Is a Size Transition?

Weighing the Giant Fly

One of my math teachers in high school was also the football coach. Mr. Clark liked to liven up the classes with some sort of action, so he showed us part of a horror movie and asked us to estimate the weight of the villain, a giant fly about 12 feet tall. To create this towering insect, the filmmakers had photographed a real housefly and showed the enlarged image standing next to human beings apparently half its height.

"Look at those legs," Mr. Clark said. "Could those legs hold up a twelve-foot fly?"

"Well, why not?" we asked.

The whole figure had been enlarged in exact proportion to the original. If the legs of the little fly were sufficient to support the body, why would it be any different for the big fly?

Suppose a real housefly is a centimeter long, a centimeter tall, and a centimeter wide. Suppose he weighs one gram. Wouldn't a fly twice as big weigh two grams? In fact, if you double all the dimensions of the fly, you will quadruple the shadow he casts on the picnic table at noon and increase eightfold the amount he weighs. Our giant fly would need thick legs like an elephant in order to stand up, and he wouldn't be much of an aviator.

When organisms change significantly in size, they must also change in form. That's just the way the world works, and the rule holds true for social as well as biological organisms. Kenneth Blanchard has shown how the number of possible interactions multiplies as a social system grows in tiny increments. With three people in a room, 11 different configurations of communication are possible: A speaks to B; A speaks to B in the presence of C; and so on. Add a fourth person and the number spikes to 54.[1]

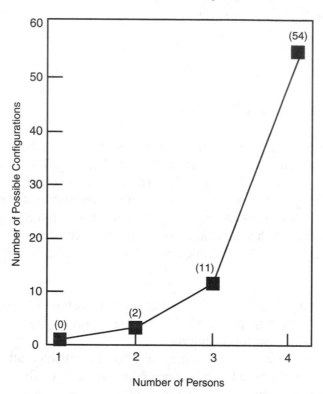

**How Complexity Grows
in Human Systems**

For the last three decades or so, students of religious systems have tried to describe the changes in *form* that must occur in order to allow a congregation to change in *size*. While there is no single agreed-upon framework for describing size differences, there is convergence of opinion regarding some key dimensions of size transition and some of the typical plateau points. These are the attendance levels at which a church, growing naturally in a conducive environment, will probably get stuck unless it undergoes a change of form.

The Ramp and the Stairs

Size transition is a powerful diagnostic concept for church leaders. There are eras in a congregation's life when attendance grows in steady increments, like walking up a ramp. These are periods of continuous change—times of steady evolution in the same direction. Most of us are skilled at responding to slow, unidirectional change in our lives. With little effort we adjust our sleep patterns to the small daily changes in the amount of daylight. We increase our purchase of coffee and sugar as the number of people at the church's social hour gradually grows.

Other periods in a congregation's life might better be described as discontinuous change—the straw that broke the camel's back. These are the moments when "just a little bit more" pushes the organism across an invisible threshold and causes previously reliable systems to break down. Instead of a ramp, we are facing a step which represents a quantum leap. It's all or nothing if we want to move forward. Several different observers[2] of church life have created frameworks to help us see where the "steps" are—the levels of attendance at which the potential for gradual change runs out and a whole new form is required if the church is to move fully into the next size. Here is one way to visualize the steps, based on the work of Arlin Rothauge; the numbers refer to average worship attendance.[3]

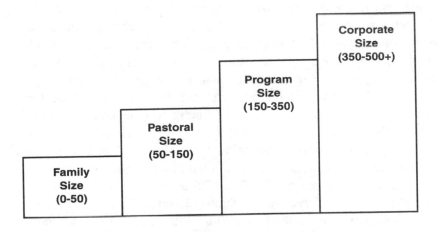

This framework has clear limitations. The threshold figure for movement into corporate size was more arbitrarily chosen than the others and may be considerably higher. Additional steps experienced by congregations over 1,000 are not included at all in the chart. Carl George's categories[4] will be more helpful in these situations, and his metachurch alternative represents a bold attempt to remove the growth barriers between sizes altogether. At the small-church end of the spectrum, an innovative approach called "total ministry"[5] steps outside Rothauge's description of family size with a more intentional structure for ministry development within the congregation.

Having noted these limitations, I would reaffirm the value of the Rothauge categories as an aid to decision making in the majority of mainline congregations today. Churches almost always encounter difficulty when they arrive at a step—the boundary between one size and the next—because the culture of the congregation is in flux. Formal and informal relationships are being reshaped; key structures and processes are changing. Such troubles emerge whether the church is moving to a larger or a smaller size. After the final chapter of this book, you will find an article by Roy Oswald describing the dynamics of ministry in churches of these four sizes. I recommend that you pause and read that appendix now. Here is a very brief review of some of the differences.

The *family size church* (up to 50 people attending) is a single-cell organism—a social system resembling an extended biological family in which "we all know each other." As in actual families, some members are added by birth or marriage, while others are incorporated rather slowly and carefully in a process of adoption. Given the small membership numbers, clergy are usually part-time and short-term in such churches. Though they are permitted to function as chaplains to the family, the leadership that actually holds these churches together comes from the matriarchs and patriarchs—anchoring figures who maintain stability through their tacit authority. A healthy, family size church is usually known in its community for one vibrant ministry focus, often some form of direct service to the community offered in a down-home style.

The *pastoral size church* (50 to 150) is a multi-cell organism— a coalition of several overlapping family-friendship networks unified around the person and role of the pastor. When a congregation is portrayed in literature, in films, or on television, it is often made in this pastoral image: a church on the green with its resident parson. At its best, this congregation is big enough to look to the visitor like a "real church," and small enough to feel personal. If the pastor is suited to the community and has a good team relationship with the board, harmony and spiritual coherence can result. Churches with attendances under 100, however, cannot usually support a full-time clergy position and may experience a lot of pastoral turnover. A healthy, pastoral size church is usually known in its community for two or three strong ministries, including worship with a personal touch.

The *program size church* (150 to 350) is known, as the name suggests, for the quality and variety of its programs. Its larger and more diverse membership will contain a "critical mass" of people from several different age and interest groups—children, youth, couples, and seniors, for example. This substantial presence of varied populations stimulates creative ministry and provides entry points for new members from different demographic groups. Typically, part- and full-time staff are added as programs are initiated or strengthened, but the ministries of members also expand into areas such as pastoral care, new member incorporation, community outreach, and the leadership of small groups for sharing and prayer about members' own life circumstances. At its best, the program size church's excellent processes for democratic participation create a sense of excitement, purpose, and possibility.

The *corporate size church* (350 to 500+) is a significant institutional presence in its community. It may have a cathedral-like building in a prominent location, associated institutions like a day school or community center, and a sizeable staff of highly skilled professionals. This larger congregation can provide "something for everybody"—a variety of different kinds of worship, education, spiritual nurture, and social interaction. It also provides a visitor the chance to remain anonymous for a while—a plus for some people in urban settings who may not want to make commitments right away. Sometimes this congregation attracts into membership key leaders from the wider community because of its substantial public presence. "Tall steeple churches" usually seek "tall steeple pastors"—clergy with a sufficient symbolic presence to focus a large worship service, head an extensive staff, and challenge powerful lay leaders with a bold and unifying purpose.

No Room at the Inn—or Too Much?

An understanding of transition dynamics between these sizes is critical
for congregations that want to offer "holy hospitality" to the people
around them who are longing for connection with God and for the experience of faith community. Most of us wouldn't dream of putting up
active barriers to potential members. Can you imagine a church with a
sign out front that says, "Not accepting new members at this time"? But
what about the "passive barriers," the subtler signs that hinder hospitality just as powerfully? Suppose there are no parking spaces visible at the
worship hour? Suppose the nursery is cramped and chaotic when the
newcomer walks in with her child? Suppose the visitor card she drops in
the offering plate is not acknowledged because the pastor is too busy to
follow up? Our welcoming intentions may be good, but the effect on that
person will be the same as if we hung out a "membership closed" sign.
At the plateau points between sizes, *many invisible hindrances converge* to prevent the assimilation of new members and the full participation of those already on our rolls.

Some congregations are facing another kind of size transition—a
movement toward forms of church life that fit a smaller number of members. Most mainline congregations have some potential for numerical
growth, even in demographically declining areas, if both the clergy and
lay opinion leaders are outreach-oriented.[6] Sometimes, however, both
spiritual and institutional health require that we relinquish the hollow
forms of the larger church we used to be. Potentially vital congregations
are often defeated by a sea of empty seats, by nostalgia for the days of
the beloved pastor, or by the ghost of programs past. Here, size transition means starting with reality and structuring for attainable growth—
not for the fantasy that the glory days will magically return.

I recently worked with a downtown congregation, housed in a cathedral-like facility, whose worship attendance had dwindled over a forty-
year period to about one hundred people. Much of this contraction was
driven by dramatic demographic changes over which the church had no
control. The decline was reinforced, however, by an unwillingness to
relinquish patterns that were appropriate to corporate size. When, for
example, a second worship service was launched using an attractive
chapel area, complaints arose from other congregants about "not using
our magnificent sanctuary" (an expression of nostalgia for the corporate

days when it was full). Though this modest-sized service would probably have increased the congregation's total attendance and provided an anchor for a different generation group, leaders capitulated and moved the service to the enormous sanctuary. Soon thereafter, it died. I would bet that this congregation has made dozens of similar decisions in recent decades, reinforcing rather than mitigating the cycle of decline by refusing to update its self-concept and ministry patterns.

Loren Mead's recent work on the financial circumstances of mainline congregations[7] shows that more and more of our smaller pastoral size churches will soon be falling below the level of income needed to retain a full-time, seminary-educated pastor. When churches move to part-time clergy (sometimes a possibility in larger metropolitan areas), they gain financial flexibility but often settle into prolonged depression and self-hatred because their definition of a "real" church is based on a pastor-centered constellation. Such feelings will reinforce and speed the decline unless the congregation can fully claim the structure and positive values of family size—including, perhaps, a more manageable facility. In more isolated areas of the country, where the calling of even part-time clergy is impossible, more innovative ministry alternatives are required.

Sometimes two or more small churches share a single pastor ("yoking"). Sometimes several covenant together to call a team of part- and full-time staff, often with an experienced supervising pastor at the helm ("cluster" or "team" ministries). Sometimes they begin talks about merger or ecumenical cooperation. Sometimes they send people for training as lay pastors or move to a more dramatically communal understanding of ministry, with special preparation and support ("total ministry"). In all these cases, the new arrangement will not result in vital church life and ministry unless the remembered patterns of pastoral size are clearly relinquished.

A major challenge for a church at the lower threshold of any size category is discerning whether it has the demographic potential, the human and financial capital, and the real desire to launch an effort at numerical growth. Although this book is not a general introduction to church growth principles and methods, it may help you to estimate what would be required to increase your membership and may point you to other relevant resources. Whichever way you decide to go—toward new effort at membership growth or toward vitality at a smaller size—your decision will be stronger if you explore the costs and values on both sides and understand what the transition will require.

Living in the Gap

Congregational life during a size transition tends to be confusing and stressful. One pattern of interaction has run its course, but a new one has not yet emerged. Members are constantly bumping into boundary phenomena—experiences that disrupt previously reliable expectations. Leaders have a hard time planning because their tools for predicting and regulating the life of the system are no longer adequate. Stresses like these will confront any church whose external environment is changing rapidly. When a small town becomes engulfed in metropolitan sprawl, for example, its churches will have to adapt to many new realities. Even in a relatively stable environment, however, reaching a size plateau will unsettle the congregation's life.

In the next chapters we will look at some of the numerical and behavioral clues that indicate if a congregation is bumping its head on the glass ceiling of a size plateau. But first, let's pause to think about what happens to people of faith when their familiar patterns are disrupted. The biblical books of Exodus and Numbers describe a period of discontinuous change in the life of the people of Israel. This discontinuity was precipitated, perhaps over a period of many years, by very bad news in the environment: the rise of a pharaoh who didn't remember Joseph's contribution to Egyptian life and so had no qualms about cruelty to the Hebrew slaves. He demanded more bricks and took away the supplies of straw the workers needed to make them.

This great period of discontinuity in Israel's life was more immediately precipitated by good news: God's call to Moses to confront the pharaoh and lead the people out of slavery. Their deliverance from slaughter and their miraculous walk across the seabed became the cornerstone of Israel's faith and ritual. But God's promise of a new pattern of life in a new land required that they first endure a period of chaos in the wilderness.

Despite the clear vision of God's purposes given to Moses, the people were frequently confused, frightened, and angry. The experience of slavery had been oppressive but predictable. Life in the wilderness, on the other hand, was terribly uncertain. Food and water were often in doubt, and they were crossing through the territory of alien peoples. Every new circumstance demanded of them a radical trust in God and a profound cooperation with their leaders.

Is God with us here, in these new circumstances? Is God powerful enough to care for us in today's unforgiving terrain? Do our leaders hear the voice of God, or only their own private dreams and desires? Do we, together, have sufficient sense of God's call to maintain our communal bonds, even as we pass through a wild frontier? These are the deep questions your congregation must struggle with in a time of size transition.

Biblical Reflection

The fifteenth chapter of Exodus describes the very beginning of the wilderness experience. In verse 21 we can still hear the tones of Miriam's song, celebrating God's mighty act of liberation. By the end of verse 22, the people have been without water for three days and are angry with Moses for bringing them out into this unknown and insecure place.

1. Read Exodus 15:20-27 and note your first reactions. If you have ever been in danger of real physical harm from lack of water, perhaps on a camping trip, recall what it was like. If not, what do you imagine it would be like to fear that you may die of thirst?

2. What thoughts and feelings might Moses have had in this first stage of the journey? What is it like to have your leadership questioned?

3. What wilderness periods has your congregation experienced in the past? Listen to the details of these stories and see if you can find a pattern in the way your church handles such experiences.

4. If you have identified that your church is in a size transition, can you name aspects that feel like wilderness? Can you think of any gifts that God has given to sustain you in this wilderness journey?

Application Exercise

Review the descriptions of the four sizes found in this chapter (pages 3-5) and in appendix A. For the moment, focus on the narrative about each size rather than on the attendance ranges. (We will look more closely at your attendance figures in chapter 2.)

1. Which of the four brief descriptions in this chapter sounds most like your congregation?

2. Now read Roy Oswald's longer discussion of the size that you chose. Would you still put your church in the same category? Why or why not?

CHAPTER 2

Are We Facing a Size Transition?

Glass Ceiling

Between sizes, congregations that have been growing steadily tend to hit an attendance plateau. Often they notice a mismatch between the attendance trend and what is occurring in other measures of growth. An expanding congregation may experience a continued increase in the number of visitors, members, pledging households, or dollars contributed, but still see a flat line on the graph of average attendance from year to year. If left unattended long enough, such a plateau will most often turn into a decline. (The chart on page 14 illustrates such a case.)

Sometimes an attendance plateau is determined primarily by community demographics. In an isolated rural community with a fixed population, virtually every resident may have a well-established pattern of religious participation (or non-participation). Life passages such as birth, marriage, childbearing, illness, and death provide the primary openings for new or deeper relationship with God. Here a faithful, lively, and inviting congregation might take in or reactivate just enough members each year to replace those who die or move away.

Sometimes a flat attendance line is caused primarily by physical factors. For example, a worship service will tend to stop growing when 80 percent of the desirable seats are occupied on a regular basis; newcomers won't come back, current members will attend less frequently, or both. When you calculate your seating capacity, keep two things in mind. First, don't count inferior seating areas (say, in the balcony) where regular members would never want to sit. Second, remember that acceptable social distance changes with the culture; pews that used to

seat five can today only be counted as space for three.[1] Some congregations can break through an attendance plateau simply by adding more
seating capacity, more parking spaces, or an additional service.[2]

In contrast to plateaus created solely by community demographics
or physical space limitations, the glass-ceiling effect of a size transition
will occur even when there are many unchurched people around and
plenty of seats left. Growth in attendance will level off because of a
shortage of "sociological space." These size-related plateaus tend to be
more mysterious to members and leaders because the causes are less
visible and more cumulative in nature. At the boundary between sizes,
many different hindrances converge to prevent the assimilation of new
members and the full participation of those already on the rolls.

The Plateau Zone

The diagram of the Rothauge categories in the previous chapter showed
the boundary between sizes as a sharp line. In fact, we see a plateau
zone between the sizes: a band in which attendance wobbles around
until there is a definite move to the next size (up or down). The first
plateau zone occurs between 50 and 70 in attendance. This is an important boundary area to understand because it could potentially affect the
growth of 70 percent of the Christian congregations in North America.[3]
The second plateau zone occurs between 150 and 200 at weekend worship. This is the ceiling that would be confronted by another quarter of
North American churches if they were to grow substantially. So, the
majority of congregations grappling with a growth plateau are stuck in
one of these two zones.

What about the other five percent of churches? A third plateau zone
seems to appear at 350 to 400, especially in congregations with an extensive plant and a large endowment helping to support staff and programs. A fourth may occur at attendances between 800 to 1,000. Less
than 1 percent of churches on this continent have broken through the
1,000 level, and only one-tenth of 1 percent have gone through the 3,000
barrier. Around the world, a handful of congregations have found a way
to grow into the tens of thousands at worship.

The point of this discussion is not to persuade you that your congregation should have 20,000 people at worship on Sunday—or even 20,

for that matter. My concern is to make apparent what may otherwise be invisible forces in the life of your congregation; to give leaders and members more choices as they seek to discern God's call together; and to offer a kind of pastoral care for congregations experiencing the frustration and ambivalence which often occur at size plateaus.

Seeing the Invisible

A crucial place to begin your exploration is with the numerical realities. This is an act of contemplation and discernment. It doesn't presuppose an answer to the question, What size are we called to be?

You will need to gather data from your worship records and calculate the yearly averages of worship attendance. Include all weekend services that do not duplicate each other's attendance. (You may, for example, have a special worship service on Sunday evenings—such as vespers or a healing service—that does not serve as the main worship occasion for any segment of the congregation. Don't count people twice.) Count all ages, even if some children are in the nursery or church school and not in the adult worship service. In congregations where a large percentage of attendance consists of children (more than a quarter of the total), you may want to break down the figures and record data for both adults and children.

For the past 10 years, figure the average for each individual year based on data for all 52 weeks. Back beyond that, you may decide to calculate averages only for every third year or fifth year to gain an impression of trends. If actual attendance counts are missing, choose the nearest year for which records exist.[4] Once you have assembled your figures, plot this data visually. Trends and transitions become apparent in a graphic representation that cannot easily be seen in the numbers themselves. Here is a sample of what one chart looks like, from an actual congregation whose case we will explore more deeply in chapter 7. For ease of explanation, I have plotted on the horizontal axis the tenure of the two most recent pastors.

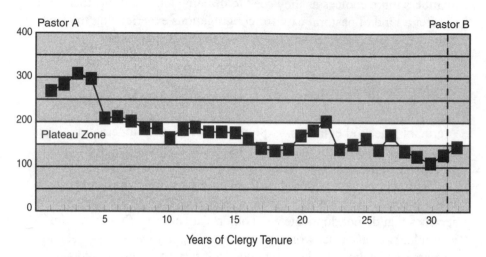

Average Attendance
St. Peter's, Seaside

Notice how the congregation in the example grew rapidly about 30 years ago to the top of program size. This peak reflected the energy of an able new pastor and the population growth occurring in the community, but attendance quickly dropped down into the pastoral-to-program plateau zone and stayed there (150 to 200) for most of the next 25 years. In the last five years, during which the pastor retired and the congregation searched for a new pastor, attendance levels dipped down into pastoral size.

God Is in the Details

Should we be so concerned about numbers? I want to turn again to the account of the wilderness experience, most of which is recorded in the part of the Scriptures called Numbers by Christians. The Hebrew title for this book refers to the journey in the wilderness, but it acquired an alternate title because the very first task on the wilderness journey was a census.

Does that seem strange? There they were in the wild borderland between their old life as slaves in Egypt and their new life in a land of promise. Was God's call to them simply about numbers? Of course not.

But the people needed to know where they stood in this time of transition, and leaders needed to assess what the journey would require. So they counted.

Numbers do not determine our vocation as congregations. As persons and as faith communities, we listen for and respond to the voice of a living God. But one way to prepare for that sacred conversation about vocation is to look carefully, with an attitude of contemplation, at the numerical facts. This requires courage. We may be afraid that the picture will depress us or cause us to be blamed for the congregation's troubles. We may be afraid that the picture will challenge us to relinquish things we hold dear. Will God be with us then? Will the pillar of cloud by day and the pillar of fire by night still go ahead of us to guide our journey? Faith says yes, even as fear says no.

Biblical Reflection

The opening chapters of the book of Numbers contain Israel's marching orders for the journey in the wilderness, beginning with a careful census of each tribe. Clearly, this is seen as essential preparation for the 40 transitional years ahead.

1. Why do you think that a census was important?

2. How do you feel about the act of recording and counting attendance?

3. How can numbers be misused?

Application Exercise

Review the third section of this chapter (Seeing the Invisible) for information about gathering attendance statistics.

1. When you have compiled your yearly averages in rough form, transfer them to one of the blank charts that follows, or to an enlarged version on flip-chart paper. Plotting the data will help you to see if there are plateaus in your church data and whether or not they match up with the predicted transition zones between sizes (represented by the

unshaded areas). The first worksheet provided is designed for family and pastoral size churches. The second is for congregations that are, or have been during the past 30 years, program or corporate size.

2. Based on attendance numbers, what size categories has your congregation experienced during the past 30 years?

3. Look at the peaks and valleys on the chart. Identify events in the life of the church, or of your surrounding community, that might correlate with those highs and lows.

4. Look for periods when the attendance line flattened out. Discuss whether you think these plateaus were most influenced by:

   a. Physical limitations, such as seating or parking
   b. Population trends in your surrounding community
   c. The glass-ceiling effect of a size transition

Worksheet A:

Chart of average weekend worship attendance during the last 30 years

(For use by family or pastoral size churches)

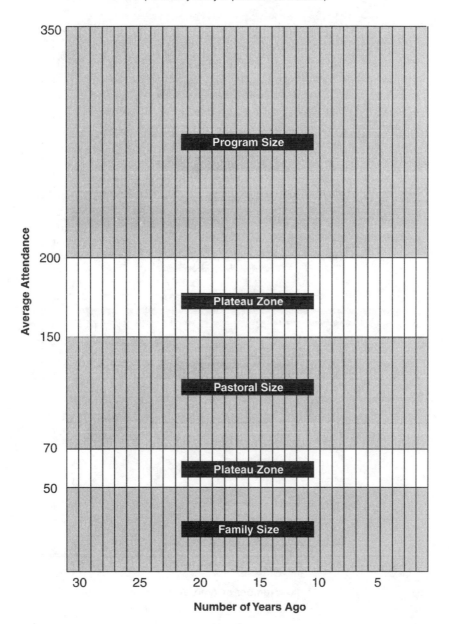

Average Attendance

350

Program Size

200

Plateau Zone

150

Pastoral Size

70

Plateau Zone

50

Family Size

30   25   20   15   10   5

Number of Years Ago

Worksheet B:

Chart of average weekend worship attendance during the last 30 years

(For use by program or corporate size churches)

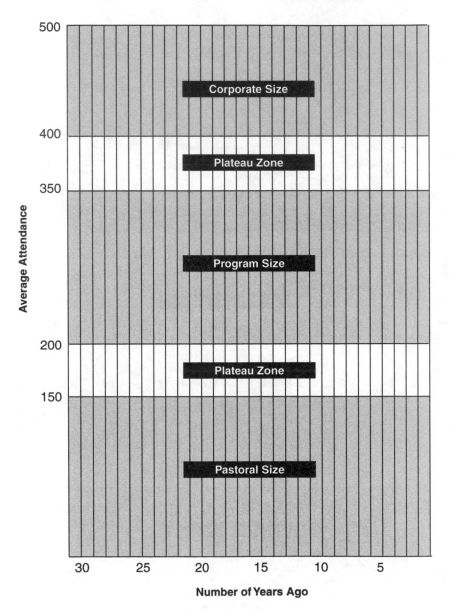

CHAPTER 3

What Happens between Sizes?

Fault Lines

My brother used to live near the San Andreas fault in California. This is a long rift in the earth's crust that periodically tears open to accommodate shifts in the two tectonic plates whose meeting creates a fault line. As a visitor to my brother's home, I used to imagine myself standing with one foot on each side of the fault, then dropping into a chasm when the earthquake hit.

Size transition is a lot like standing on the fault line. You can make better decisions if you know not only where the rifts occur but also what deeper movements of the earth are driving the surface eruption. Congregations are changing and adjusting all the time. Dozens of different factors are in play, and subtle gradations exist that make any size theory look oversimplified. Still, some of the forces at work are more powerful than others, more determinative of relationships and results. For the majority of congregations,[1] a two-dimensional model of size change will clarify the lines of demarcation.

One dimension of change, shown along the bottom of the following chart, is described by the terms *organism* and *organization*. The other dimension is described by the terms *pastor-centered* and *group-centered*. Churches moving through the plateau zones on the graphs in the last chapter are actually crossing fault lines on this topographical map. As congregations move among Rothauge's four sizes—family, pastoral, program, and corporate—they follow an N-shaped path across the fault lines.

Size Transition "N-Curve"

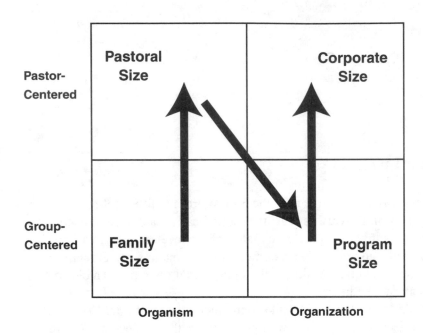

Organism versus Organization

Pastor-Centered

Pastoral Size

Corporate Size

Group-Centered

Family Size

Program Size

Organism   Organization

Organism versus Organization

Family and pastoral size churches resemble an organism more than an organization. Congregations of these two sizes tend to be relatively homogeneous in make-up. Each revolves around a central relationship that can be immediately and intuitively apprehended: the relationship among members as a "primary group" or "single cell" (family size church) or the dyadic relationship between the sole ordained leader and the congregation (pastoral size church). The congregation's identity is largely inherent in these central relationships. Ask the question "Who are you as a church?" in a family size congregation, and someone will probably introduce you around the whole circle of members. Ask that question in a pastoral size church, and someone will most likely tell you about the congregation's relationship with its pastor, often symbolized by the rapport (or lack thereof) between pastor and board. In these two smaller sizes, the notion that a congregation might choose or shape an identity intentionally would probably seem odd; identity is more of a given, to be preserved and defended.

In program and corporate size churches, on the other hand, the variety and complexity of relationships require conscious attention to matters of identity, purpose, structure, role of leaders, and so on. Neither the members nor the pastor can intuitively grasp the wholeness of the system. The larger membership and the rich variety of programming will only cohere well if leaders construct a clear identity for the church— often expressed in a mission statement, a vision, or a strategic plan. For people raised in smaller churches, this work of construction may seem taxing and bureaucratic. On the other hand, the quest for intentionality typical of a larger congregation might stimulate their imagination about church life, clarify their reasons for participation, and provide richer networks of friendship, growth, and ministry. Membership is more of a choice than a given.

The distinction between organism and organization is not absolute. Small congregations are still subject to the laws that govern not-for-profit corporations in the United States and may be vulnerable to lawsuits if they do not attend well to organizational matters like the employment, accountability, and termination of staff. Larger congregations are still living systems, held together by subtly balanced forces which we may only dimly perceive. Nevertheless, the difference between the two emphases is usually palpable.

Group-Centered versus Pastor-Centered

The movement from family to pastoral size (the upward arrow on the left-hand side of the chart on page 20) involves a change in the way the system centers its life. The family size church feels like a tribe or a committee of the whole. Not everyone on the committee has equal influence, to be sure, but the single cell of members works things through in its own characteristic way. A student minister or part-time pastor who tries to take charge of that cell is in for a rude awakening because a family size church does not generally revolve around the pastor.[2]

At a worship attendance of about 35 people, that single cell of membership becomes stretched. By the time it hits 50, the unbroken circle of members—that defining constellation of the congregation's life—is in crisis. In order to increase further, the system must allow itself to become a multi-cell organism, holding together two or three overlapping networks of family and fellowship. And it must establish a symbolic center around which those multiple cells can orient themselves. Typically, it becomes pastor-centered.

A great deal has been written about the dangers of clerical domination in churches, and many have questioned whether this shift to a pastor-centered system is desirable at all. I would not equate "pastor-centered" with "pastor-dominated." The research of Speed Leas and George Parsons suggests that a greater proportion of members may actually participate in decisions at pastoral size than at family size.[3] It may be that the heightened role of the pastor in relation to the board moves the congregation's political center from the kitchen table to a more accessible public setting and requires that the ordained and elected leaders work as a team to move projects forward. The pastor's central position as communication switchboard also allows for a great deal of informal consultation and problem solving; he or she can monitor key relationships, initiate needed conversations, and anticipate likely clashes.

As attendance approaches 150, however, the congregation must become more group-centered once again because the pastor can no longer carry around the whole system in his or her head. There are too many individual, pastoral needs to track. The relationships among projects and leaders are becoming too complex to be coordinated solely through board discussion and pastoral diplomacy. A new kind of teamwork becomes necessary in an uneven leadership matrix in which some programs have paid staff, some have volunteer leaders so dedicated that they function like staff, and some have committees at the helm. Board and pastor must find ways to keep the parts connected with each other *directly*—in horizontal networks of collaboration—not just *indirectly* through board reports and liaisons. As in a spider web, the center of this leadership network does not consist of a single point (the pastor) but of a small circle (half a dozen key program leaders–paid and unpaid, clergy and lay) led by the pastor.

In the move to program size, clergy must shift a good deal of their time and attention away from the direct delivery of pastoral care and focus on assembling and guiding that small team of program leaders. They must also find ways to offer spiritual enrichment to the board, whose job has become much more demanding. Skills for this kind of group-oriented ministerial leadership have not usually been emphasized in seminary or employed as primary selection criteria in the ordination process. Hence, many clergy find themselves poorly equipped for a pastoral-to-program transition.

To make things worse, the breakdown of the pastor-centered way of being a church occurs at the same time as the shift from organism to organization. The congregation is now traversing the diagonal portion of the N-shaped path, crossing both the horizontal and vertical fault lines simultaneously. The pastoral-to-program change is doubly discontinuous.

When attendance reaches about 350, the need for more pastor-centered leadership emerges once again. (Note the vertical line on the right-hand side of the chart.) The program church's lively but lumpy network of staff, volunteer program heads, and committees can no longer provide the overview and strategic direction the system needs. At corporate size, complex networks of coordination are still required, but the central pastor must begin to project a large enough symbolic presence—through preaching, presiding, leading the board, and heading the expanded staff—to unify a diverse and energetic community. To be effective, this high-profile leader must find a reliable way to maintain spiritual perspective and must use the aura of headship to help the whole system grapple with its core identity and purpose.

Six Transitions

It may be helpful to summarize some critical issues that must be addressed during the six possible transitions within the Rothauge framework. The placement of each movement on the N-curve is shown.

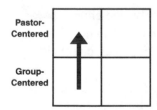

Family-to-Pastoral Transition

- Loss of self-esteem by matriarchs and patriarchs as they lose decisive influence in the system: Can they be helped to pass the mantle, with pride in the past during which they presided?

- Tendency for unseasoned clergy to take resistance personally: How can congregations find mature pastoral leadership? How can less experienced clergy find mentors to help them handle their own insecurities?

- Reluctance to divide the single cell: How can current leadership weigh what may be gained and lost as they relinquish the expectation that every event (Sunday worship, study programs, Christmas Eve service) must include the whole family?

- Financial realism: Clergy salaries and benefits are rising in most denominations. Can the congregation move solidly enough into pastoral size to attain stability?

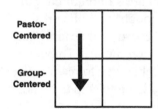

Pastoral-to-Family Transition

- Loss of self-esteem by congregation when it feels it is no longer operating like a "real" church: Will the move signal slow death, or will something new and vigorous begin?

- Ministry development: How will gifts be discerned and developed for a rich variety of home-grown ministries?

- Support and accountability: How will the family size church partner with its denomination (or with parachurch organizations) to monitor the development of sound ministries and open channels to other congregations, leaders, and ideas?

- Physical plant: What is an appropriate facility for this church? Does worship need to be moved so that the space will be at least half full on Sunday (the minimum required to attract newcomers)?

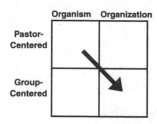

Pastoral-to-Program Transition

- Clergy role: Will leaders recognize the double messages they are giving the clergy about what they expect? (Try the "A-B" exercise in Roy Oswald's article.) Will clergy work on resolving their personal ambivalence about these choices and on gaining the new skills they need? How will staff be augmented to allow for growth?

- Program leadership: How will gifted and motivated people be selected, equipped, and authorized to serve as department heads? Does the pastor have the skills needed to forge these heads into a staff team? Who will help the average member identify gifts for ministry (inside and outside the congregation), and who will make sure that every form of volunteer service to the congregation is a spiritually rewarding experience?

- Communication: How can people involved in implementing different programs stay personally connected with leaders from other programs? Will formal information channels (newsletter, bulletin, spoken announcements, telephone trees) be improved and intensified, so that timely, accurate, and thorough communication is the norm?

- Democratic participation: What channels will be provided so that every member can have a say and a stake in the shape of church life? How will members remain aware of, and accountable to, a central purpose?

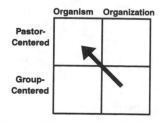

Program-to-Pastoral Transition

- Reshaping expectations: How will the congregation refocus on a few central strengths? Will there be attention to the sense of loss and grief that may accompany a consolidation of energies?

- Clergy role: What satisfactions and status must the pastor relinquish? How will simpler patterns of pastoral care be established?

- Sunday morning: How can the worship and education schedule be made manageable without reinforcing a cycle of decline? Can the church maintain at least two worship options of somewhat different styles?

- Ministry development: Healthy pastoral size churches still foster active lay leadership, especially in new-member incorporation, education, and community outreach. How will the pastor shift to a less formal style of delegation and mentoring? How will the number of committees be reduced in favor of small, hands-on ministry teams?

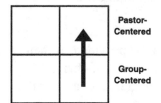

Program-to-Corporate Transition

- Depth and quality of programming: How will the church step up to a higher level of expectations? Do staff members need new posi-tion descriptions (focused on empowering others for ministry) and a definite plan to gain new skills?

- Symbolic presence of central pastor: Is the senior minister ready to step into a lonelier, more spiritually hazardous role? Will he or she put in place new disciplines such as regular spiritual guidance, adequate time for sermon preparation, and use of third-party help in planning, conflict, and staff development? Who will mentor the central pastor around new and difficult responsibilities (personnel issues, endowment, delegation)?

- Strategic direction: In a system as hard to turn as an ocean liner, how will senior pastor and central board keep their focus on the big questions about the church's purpose and role? How will they engage the rest of the system in those questions without abdicating leadership?

- Small group connection: Will the congregation establish an excellent pattern of small group ministry through which members can connect faith with daily life? Will small group leaders be trained through apprenticeship so that the more experienced leaders can constantly be forming new groups?

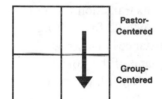

Pastor-
Centered

Group-
Centered

Corporate-to-Program Transition

- Relinquishing status: Will the church be honest about its decline and resist the temptation simply to keep up appearances?

- Use of endowment: Is the church steadily spending down the gifts of the past, rather than facing the need to consolidate programs and to develop a relevant approach to evangelism?

- Cavernous buildings: Does the sea of empty seats reinforce the cycle of decline and undermine the vitality that could be developed?

- Clergy role: Can the central pastor establish a more collegial relationship with the major program leaders and help the board to take

back the spiritual leadership which may have been relinquished in
the past to a small group of trustees?

In the case of impending transition to a smaller size, each congregation
will need to assess its growth potential and outreach commitments. Don't
reconfigure for the smaller size if you intend to move through the plateau zone within the next couple of years.

The Double-Minded Church

A classic prayer asks for the grace to love and serve God "with gladness
and singleness of heart." Both joy and single-mindedness start to run
short in a size transition; they are replaced by profound ambivalence.
Once a church has entered the plateau zone, the strength and appeal of
the previous size are already compromised, while the virtues of the next
size are not yet in place. Leaders find themselves in a lose-lose position
because two competing sets of expectations are laid upon them. Confusion, anxiety, and indecision often result.

Some of the most poignant passages in Exodus and Numbers describe the ambivalence of the faith community in its transition from the
land of bondage to the land of promise. When the people first left Egypt,
they were so daunted by their transitional circumstances that some of
them wished aloud, "If only we had died by the hand of the Lord in the
land of Egypt, when we sat by the fleshpots and ate our fill of bread"
(Exod. 16:3).

Once they had received the Law and moved on from Sinai, they
even began to remember *Egypt* as a place flowing with milk and honey
—a description usually reserved for the promised land. Their attention
constantly drifted from God's mighty acts to the most domestic of details: "We remember the fish we used to eat in Egypt for nothing, the
cucumbers, the melons, the leeks, the onions, and the garlic; but now our
strength is dried up, and there is nothing at all but this manna to look at"
(Num. 11:5-6).

In the next chapter we will look more at questions of ambivalence
and discernment, but the following Biblical Reflection questions may
help you get in touch with your own inner conflicts about size transition.

Biblical Reflection

1. Read Numbers 10:33 to 11:9. Why do you think the passage from Numbers talks about food in such detail?

2. Can you imagine yourself wanting to go back to Egypt? Why or why not?

3. As your church considers issues of size transition, what do you already miss that might be comparable to the Israelites' longing for savory smells from their kitchens in Egypt?

4. If your congregation moved solidly to next size (smaller or larger, depending on your circumstances), what do you imagine to be the greatest loss you personally would have to deal with?

Application Exercise

1. Which, if any, of the six transitions discussed on pages 23 to 28 is your church experiencing?

2. Review the critical issues (bulleted items) which commonly accompany that particular transition. To what extent has your congregation encountered each of these issues? What other issues have you experienced as a result of your change in size?

CHAPTER 4

Should We Be Growing?

Opening Up the Conversation

We believe in a God to whom "all hearts are open, all desires known." [1] Sometimes we have a lot of work to do—uncovering the desires of our own hearts—before we can hear clearly what God may desire for us. An incarnational spirituality requires that we engage in prayerful dialogue with our own longings.

As you ponder your congregation's call regarding size and numerical growth, you may find it helpful to map out the yearnings that are imbedded in this choice.

At all three points on the map, the Spirit of God is working. All of our individual desires, if we trace them back far enough, are rooted in the goodness of creation and oriented toward union with God. To be sure, they become distorted. What once was called idolatry is now more commonly called addiction: placing something essentially good (food, drink, sex, money, work, approval) at the very center of our lives. Whenever we try to fill the "God-shaped hole" in our being with something other than God, we confuse the giver with the gift, investing ultimate trust in persons or things too fragile to bear that weight. Even so, each longing is rooted in the subsoil of our God-given humanness.

As the congregation wrestles with the possibility of growth, it is important to create space where leaders and members can explore their own particular desires in this matter and recognize the conflicts that exist even within themselves. Right now I am excited by the steady growth happening in the parish I recently joined, but I am also apprehensive about the changes that may be required as we welcome others. Part of me wants to "haul up the gangplank" now that I'm on board. Part of me does not believe that there is enough grace and love and sacrament to go around.

Clergy have an especially tough time admitting their own resistance to growth. It is much easier to project ambivalence on others—pinning the problem on parish old-timers, on the denomination's mistakes, or on the heathen attitudes of the next generation. There are plenty of reasons a pastor might dread the spiritual and political demands of a size transition. Although some clergy are simply not suited to this kind of ministry, almost any ordained leader will experience conflicting desires about growth.

A congregation approaching size decisions needs many safe settings —over a period of months and years—for members and leaders to ponder the voices they hear in their own hearts and minds. Quiet days, study groups, and workshops with leaders from other congregations can help. By whatever means may fit your context, ask people to trace their own longings back to the very deepest desires of their hearts. If, like the Israelites, they miss the smell of onions cooking, ask them to write down in a journal all the associations they have with that smell. What memories do those onions evoke? What values do they symbolize? How could the memories and values—and perhaps the onions themselves!—be honored on the wilderness journey and planted in the new land?

The Movement from "I" to "We"

As leaders and members begin to inhabit their personal desires[2] and to share these openly with others, they may be ready to recognize the conflicting voices resonating within the congregation's corporate personality. What do *we* desire together? This question cannot be answered through the mathematics of a vote or survey, although there may come a point, after much conversation and prayer, when testing the waters with a survey or poll will be a clarifying step. Like Israel, we have a *communal* relationship with God that both embodies and transcends all our individual faith journeys. At this corner of the triangle, we are challenged to accept that the ambivalence belongs to *us together*, even though different segments of the community may vocalize particular strands of the conversation. Safe space is needed once again in order to explore all dimensions of the decision without premature recourse to debate and formal deliberation; a prayer vigil might be appropriate.[3]

When a congregation changes size, its culture and style will also change to some extent, and these are not simple matters. Sometimes we talk about sticking to the gospel and not letting "mere" matters of culture and style get in the way. Linda Clark's research into debates about church music[4] has helped me to understand that style is not a peripheral matter. There is no generic, culture-free Christianity. Every revelation of spiritual truth is embedded in a specific context, and every expression of faith has a distinctive style.

Even the bedrock proclamation of Christian faith—the gospel—is plural in context and style. Though Matthew, Mark, Luke, and John all strive to express the central news, each uses the idiom of a particular cultural setting and each conveys religious meaning in a characteristic style. We would never mistake the long strings of "thou in me and I in thee" for Mark, nor could we rewrite John in terse Marcan prose and still retain the full character of the message. Add Paul to the mix; add the early church's matriarchs and patriarchs; add the witnesses of faith down through the centuries—*nowhere* will we find a generic faith that can be separated absolutely from its cultural context and expressive style. So, if we are to clarify what *we together* desire, it helps to explore the deeply significant context and style in which the faith of this congregation has been formed.[5]

God Outside the Box

Once we come to recognize the sources of our congregation's unique character and aspirations, we will be faced with the offer—and challenge—of transformation. Though God has been active in the formation of "my desire" and "our desire," the third corner of the triangle never collapses into the other two. The transcendent One maintains a holy otherness; the living God has something new to say to us and to the world. This is the place for the distinctive task of communal discernment, by which I mean the processes Christians of different traditions have employed through the ages as they have grappled with the third corner of the triangle.[6]

"What does God desire for us now?" Though it has been more traditional to ask, "What is God's will?" I find the language of desire more compelling and more integrative. I can remember a moment 20 years ago when I read an article in a women's magazine about spiritual growth. It was a profile of President Jimmy Carter's sister, Ruth Carter Stapleton, who was at that time an active evangelist and public speaker. The interviewer had asked her about the problem many women were beginning to have with the language of "submission to God's will," especially at a point in their lives when they felt called to take more responsibility for their own decisions. Stapleton's spiritual advice still lies emblazoned in my memory: *Simply pray that you will come to desire what God desires.* This prayer for transformation is the only real resolution to our ambivalence about growth.

Listening to the Other

One powerful way we can listen for the voice of "God as Other" is to contemplate the "other" who is nearer at hand. This might occur informally through attentive neighborhood walks and quiet conversations. It might also take the form of a more structured demographic study, supplemented by interviews with a spectrum of community leaders. However it occurs, such an effort only bears spiritual fruit to the extent that we open ourselves to the otherness of our neighbors, allowing the stories of their lives to break through our self-absorption.

Contemplation is a stance in which we behold something or someone else, relinquishing any attempt to change, use, or manipulate them. In theologian Martin Buber's terms, contemplation establishes an "I-Thou" relationship. Although I don't find the critique entirely fair, some people object to various methods of church growth precisely because they may turn the other person into an object to be acquired ("getting a new member") or adjusted ("making a convert"). If, on the other hand, we can find a way to open ourselves to the daily reality of the people who live around us—in their own terms—then we may find our individual and corporate desires gradually transformed. At the end of this book you will find an article I have written about the use of community demographics to contemplate the other and seek God's desire for your congregation.

So . . . Should We Be Growing?

We have circled back around to this chapter's central question. Community statistics cannot answer for you the question of your church's vocation in its particular place and time. But a careful exploration of community realities will stimulate holy imagination and break open new questions about your congregation's potential role in people's lives.

A simple way to begin is with a pin map of the households that comprise your congregation. It helps to use different-colored pins for people who joined the congregation in different eras, and especially for those persons who have begun attending in the last few years. The way the colors cluster often tells a story about how people were drawn to your church in the past and how they are being drawn now. When you have finished placing the pins, ask yourself whether your map was big enough to describe your congregation's real area of ministry. If you had a group of pins leftover for households off the edge of the map, extend your map to include them all (with the exception of those who have moved a long distance away).

Once the broad ministry area is defined, mark off that radius around the church that would include half your households. Mark off a second radius that would encompass 95 to 100 percent of the households. For some churches, the two circles defined in this way will be quite similar to each other. For others, the neighborhood dimension of ministry and the wider or regional dimension may be dramatically different. This picture is part of what shapes your congregation's character and its opportunities for outreach.

Ask a team to study the demographic realities of your nearer and wider ministry area. Is it growing or declining in overall population? How is the makeup of the population changing? How closely does the membership of your congregation match the composition of your community? What are the biggest physical and social changes occurring in your ministry area?

Now comes the moment when we try to step away from the bottom of the "desire triangle," when we try to feel the heat of God's desire for us and for the people around us. Ask yourselves, "Who in this community is God trying to reach?" This isn't a one-time question, a step in a mechanical process. Rather, it is a stance you can practice until it begins to feel more natural to the parish personality. Who is God especially concerned about in your community? "Everyone" is a true but inadequate answer.

We may resist asking whom God is seeking because we are afraid of becoming overwhelmed, buried in a level of responsibility we cannot possibly bear. If you experience that fear, notice it. Name it. Write it in your journal. Share it with your study group. Most of all, offer it back to God in prayer.

Our prayers at moments like this don't have to be polite. When the people wanted to exchange the gracious bread of their freedom for the onions and leeks of Egypt, Moses had some complaints of his own about unbearable responsibility, and he put these complaints bluntly before God. "Did I conceive all this people? Did I give birth to them, that you should say to me, 'Carry them in your bosom, as a nurse carries a sucking child. . .'? I am not able to carry all this people alone, for they are too heavy for me. If this is the way you are going to treat me, put me to death at once. . . ." (Num.11:11-15). God's response to this loud objection is generous and practical—God spreads out the spirit onto 70 additional leaders. Your congregation is not the only vehicle of God's caring; you can survive the heat of God's desire if you ask for the help that you need.

Biblical Reflection

The people of Israel never went forward in the wilderness as long as the way was clouded; until God provided a clear direction, they waited and watched and prayed.

1. Read Numbers 11:15-23. Why do you think that passage is so repetitive?

2. Can you identify a time in your own life when clarity was slow in coming? What helped you stick to the process of discernment until a direction became clear?

3. Outline the particular steps your congregation has gone through so far, as it seeks to discern the desire of God. What missing steps may be clouding your decision?

4. Who in your surrounding community is God trying to reach? Is God providing any hints about which of those people your congregation has the gifts and vocation to reach?

Application Exercise

Using the information in the final section of this chapter (So . . . Should We Be Growing?), create a pin map of member households. Then discuss the following questions:

1. What are the rough boundaries of your church's current ministry area?

2. Look at the inner radius (area that includes about half your households). What are the characteristics of that area, both geographic and demographic?

3. Look at the wider radius. In what ways does the outer ring differ from the inner circle geographically and demographically?

4. As you look at the pin colors, describe any patterns you notice. From where has your congregation drawn people in the past? From where do you draw people now?

5. Using a purchased demographic profile (as described in appendix **B**) or information from your municipal planning department, describe the demographic trends in your overall ministry area:

   a. How much has the population of this area grown or declined in the past decade?
   b. What patterns are projected for the next decade?
   c. How has the makeup of the population changed during the past 10 years?
   d. How is the makeup of the population projected to change?

6. Using this information, try to expand your answer to question 4 in the Biblical Reflection. What additional groups in the population might your congregation try to reach?

CHAPTER 5

Why Make the Sacrifice?

Resolving Internal Tensions

If size transition is such a challenging project, why would a congregation like yours consider attempting it? There are a variety of answers, and they fall into three general categories: internal problem solving, mission strategy, and spiritual growth. Let's start with internal tensions as a motivation for engaging the work of size transition.

In my own training and consulting practice, church leaders frequently ask me to work with them on transition issues after they have heard me discuss the anxiety and frustration that characterize an in-between church. They recognize themselves in that description and begin to interpret their experience through the concepts of size transition. In almost every situation of this kind, I hear expressions of profound relief from lay leaders and clergy: "So *that's* what's wrong around here!" "It's not just us; other congregations have these problems, too!"

Talking explicitly about size transition brings new anxieties, to be sure. Congregations in the plateau zone have often been working very hard (perhaps in a subconscious way) to keep the possibility of significant numerical growth off the agenda. When, for example, a church's seats are mostly filled on a typical Sunday, it would seem rational to plan for extending the building or adding a new worship service. I find it remarkably unusual, however, to find a plateau church that is working steadily on some specific plan to expand the physical or sociological space for newcomers.

Often, such discussions have been nipped in the bud by adamant assertions about "sacrificing quality," "losing the character of the building," or "creating division if we add a service." Since most of us—

especially clergy and church board members—dislike conflict, our most natural response to a plateau is either to pretend that it isn't there (some congregations avoid attendance statistics like the plague) or to imagine that it will shortly go away on its own. In a Lutheran study of stable and declining congregations in the United States, 86 percent of the congregations in the sample expected their membership to remain stable or to grow, in spite of the evident trends.

It takes a great deal of energy to avoid dealing with issues that are right in front of us. This work of denial may have some initial value, such as postponing change until the issues have ripened and the change proposals have matured into a relatively coherent plan.[1] However, remaining in this mode very long will sap vitality and eventually precipitate a decline through two methods I call "war" and "pestilence." Congregations in the plateau zone are inherently unstable, their coherence strained by numbers which cannot be fully incorporated using their current configuration of ministry. When a congregation lacks a shared conceptual framework about size or an adequate process for discussing growth options, it will probably resolve the tensions of the plateau zone less consciously.

War and Pestilence

One option is war—a nasty fight (sometimes over an apparently trivial matter) which depresses attendance and discourages newcomers. Another option is pestilence—some form of illness or misbehavior which will have the same effect on numbers. While church life doesn't "cause" alcoholism, misdirected intimacy, or heart attacks in church leaders, a sustained denial (or ignorance) of size-related problems may put leaders under enormous duress and trigger the onset of those disorders to which they are already most susceptible. Frequently, war and pestilence do resolve the immediate crisis of growth, but they do so at enormous cost: to the individual leaders whose vulnerability is exposed; to the members (long-term and newer) who are driven away; and to the depressed and demoralized congregation that remains.

So, one powerful reason many church leaders begin studying the possibility of size transition is to head off the breakdown that may arise from the tensions of the plateau zone and to liberate the energy now bound up in avoidance, general discontent, or sheer confusion. An immediate benefit of such study is the new interpretation it provides for the stress and discomfort that the congregation and its leaders have been experiencing. Clergy start to see an alternative to the perpetual guilt they feel. Laity get excited about the important role they are called to play in order to bring about an intentional change; this process often energizes a somewhat younger generation of leaders who have learned relevant organizational skills on the job or through civic involvement. Congregational leaders as a whole may feel reassured that other churches have faced the same growth crisis, have navigated through a period of learning and debate, and have launched a new era of ministry.

Sometimes the pain of the plateau phenomenon is not widely distributed within the congregation. The pastor and a few lay leaders may be taking all the tensions into themselves, straining to fulfill two contradictory sets of expectations—and more or less succeeding because of unusual personal talents, overwork, neglect of their families, or all three. Here, full acknowledgment of the difficulty will be postponed until either a leadership transition or a breakdown occurs.

Mission Strategy

A second reason for facing the challenge of size transition is strategic and focuses more on missionary opportunities than on problems. The biggest cost of the plateau phenomenon is usually being paid by persons who are literally or figuratively invisible to the congregation. It is paid by the family who never gets in the door for their first visit because there is no parking place near the building; by the newcomer who can't stop feeling like a visitor because the "slots" in this church's social system are all filled up; or by the recent transfer who fills out the time-talent survey but never receives an invitation to serve. Occasionally, these invisible losses break through to consciousness. I know of one small church that was stunned at the end of the year to find that the average attendance hadn't changed, although they had welcomed a dozen individuals and families while losing only a few to death, transfer, or the inactive list. At that point they were forced to think about what was happening to frequency of attendance. Even though they had no written record of attendance patterns for individual members, they were still able to identify a group of long-term members who were now attending somewhat less frequently because of scarce pew space, and they were able to identify many newer members who were still at the edge because the part-time pastor didn't have time to fully welcome them.

These less visible costs will only be seen by leaders—at the level of the congregation or denomination—who believe in the potential of this church to reach further into its community. Looking at a plateau from this point of view, one would ask, "What size church(es) in this locality could best reach persons who are longing deep down to be connected with God and with a faith community?" Lyle Schaller argues that planting new congregations has always been the primary strategy for church growth in the United States, except in recent decades when denominations have shifted their attention to the growth of existing churches.[2] Speaking from the perspective of his European and worldwide research, German missiologist Christian Schwartz[3] has noted that smaller congregations may, on the whole, be more capable of new-member incorporation than larger ones, although his research does not examine either the permeability of churches at a size plateau or the preference of younger Americans for larger churches. In any case, starting a new congregation may be the most effective form of outreach in a particular location, and existing congregations will often benefit from examining this possibility alongside the option of changing sizes.

In many settings, perhaps in most, neither the congregation nor the denominational office is equipped to plant a viable new church. In these situations, the only realistic way to make space for others is to engage in the work of size transition.

Spiritual Growth

The third and deepest reason your congregation might choose to grapple with the challenge of a size transition has to do with spiritual vitality. At a plateau point, someone is apt to say, "We're interested in spiritual growth, not mere numbers." But as it turns out, matters like hospitality and outreach orientation are quality-of-life issues as well; spiritual growth and numerical growth are close cousins that tend to show up in the same congregations. Paying attention to others outside ourselves— reaching out in ministries both of service and of invitation—tends to enlarge the heart and soul of a congregation. Turning away from those outside, or limiting our concern tightly to one form of outreach while shunning the other, will soon constrict and deaden a congregation's internal life.

Two research studies underscore the relationship between the quality of a congregation's internal ministries and its openness to numerical growth. The *Church Membership Initiative* [4] reviewed and analyzed several decades of research from many different sources. As a result, it was able to distinguish three attitudes toward outreach and describe the consequences of each stance. Congregations in the first group (perhaps 20 to 30 percent of the total) are outreach-oriented in both their self-concept and their behavior. "Meeting needs in the community" turns up often in their descriptions of their congregational life. Working from a strong sense of their own faith tradition, they search for ways to share that historic faith in a changing world.

Congregations in the second group (30 to 40 percent of the total) express an interest in gaining new members, but have neither a mission-centered self-image nor specific outreach methods to translate their interest into action. They are hesitant to make the changes that might be needed to reach others in their community. A third group of churches (about 40 percent of the congregations) is clearly focused on caring for their current members. New people are welcomed to the extent that they are prepared to fit into existing patterns and activities.

Though a concern for "quality over quantity" is most likely to be articulated in the last two groups of churches,[5] the actual results are paradoxical. Congregations that focus *outward* (in both service and invitation) have the fullest *internal* life, as measured by the richness and variety of programs and ministries. They have the fewest financial difficulties, and are most likely to grow—not only in total membership, but also in the number of previously unchurched persons incorporated into their life. On the other hand, *both* of the other groups tend to report less variety and richness in their internal life, more financial problems, static or declining numbers, few previously unchurched members, and a "poor me" self-concept.

A separate study by Christian Schwarz[6] sheds more light on the relationship between quantity and quality. The instinct to focus on *quality-building* goals rather than on numerical targets is correct, he says—but it is very hard work to move from self-congratulatory rhetoric toward disciplined assessment and action. His organization in Germany, the

Institute for Church Development, has developed rather rigorous tools for measuring eight "quality characteristics": an empowering style of pastoral leadership, gift-oriented lay ministry, passionate spirituality, functional structures, inspiring worship, small groups which relate faith to life, need-oriented evangelism, and loving relationships. Schwarz uses the analogy of a farmer who does regular soil testing to determine what missing nutrients may curb the potential crop. A congregation is likely to grow "naturally," he says, if it regularly identifies and takes steps to bolster the weakest factor on the list.

A Life Poured Out

These two quite different studies agree on several fundamental points. First, quality and numerical growth are likely to coincide, though the potential for numerical growth will be greatly influenced by the congregation's community context and by the dynamics of the wider culture.[7] Second, healthy congregations keep outreach right at the center of their self-understanding. (Note that need-oriented evangelism is one of Schwarz's quality characteristics; de-emphasizing numerical goals does not mean de-emphasizing evangelism as a central aspect of congregational life.) Third, both qualitative and quantitative growth require change and risk. Both the Lutheran study and Schwarz's work highlight the way vital churches doggedly eliminate barriers and refuse to equate their faith tradition with "traditionalism." Healthy congregations are not afraid to use new words and methods, or to organize church life in innovative ways.

All the sophisticated statistics take us back to a gospel paradox. We cannot nurture our members' spiritual growth unless we also focus attention on those beyond ourselves. Congregations unwilling to pour out their life in response to God's call are unlikely to experience deep joy or the peace that passes understanding. This is the mystery of *kenosis*, the generosity of a "self-emptying" God (Phil. 2:7).

Biblical Reflection

Kenosis is the Greek term for Christ's "pouring out" of his life, or "emptying himself" on the cross; it is based on a verb used by Paul in the second chapter of the letter to the Philippians (verse 7).

1. Read Philippians 2:1-11. If possible, read or sing the paraphrase of this passage in the hymn, "All Praise to Thee, for Thou, O King Divine," with text by F. Bland Tucker.

2. Think about the history of your congregation. Identify moments when your congregation has engaged in some act of self-emptying love—risking its own comfort or security in order to follow Christ. Name some individuals who have done so.

3. What would have to be poured out or relinquished now in order for your congregation to be responsive to God's call to grow (either in numbers or in honesty about numerical decline)?

Application Exercise

1. Three motivations for attempting a size transition are described in this chapter. How would you rate these items as current motivators for your congregation's leaders and members:

	High	Medium	Low
Resolving internal tensions	____	____	____
Mission strategy	____	____	____
Spiritual growth	____	____	____

2. Review the final section (A Life Poured Out) of this chapter. Discuss your response to each of the three conclusions I have drawn from research studies:

   a. Quality and numerical growth are likely to coincide.
   b. Healthy congregations keep outreach—both invitation and service—right at the center of their self-understanding.

   c. Both qualitative growth and quantitative growth require change
and risk.

3. How would you assess your congregation's readiness to take on the
challenge of changing size? Discuss the reasons for your rating.

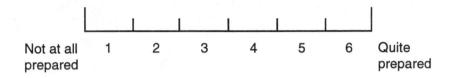

Not at all   1   2   3   4   5   6   Quite
prepared   prepared

CHAPTER 6

Should We Add a New Worship Service?

A Key Decision

If you believe that moving through a size transition is the faithful thing to do, you will need to look at the number and type of worship opportunities you are providing. Based on his research with North American Protestant churches, church growth specialist Charles Arn has concluded that about half our congregations are good candidates for adding a new worship opportunity of a somewhat different style: "Of churches that do begin a new service, eight out of ten will experience a *measurable increase* in 1) total worship attendance, 2) total giving, and 3) number of Christian conversions."[1]

Which half of the congregations are good candidates? Arn says it is easier to describe the situations in which adding a service is *not* a good bet. Don't try to add a service if the church's top priority is "community" (bringing everyone together at the same time for weekly worship), correct theology, or survival. And don't try to do it when the primary pastor is planning to leave in the next year or so. In the great majority of other churches, adding a service will foster overall growth.

Many of the assumptions that discourage church leaders from trying a new service were found to be invalid. For example, it is not true that small churches can't add worship opportunities—a church with an attendance of 40 or more is big enough to start a second service. Nor is it true that only growing churches should add a worship service; indeed, decline is an even stronger signal to try something new.

Further, leaders often assume that they should only start an additional service when the sanctuary is full.[2] Arn found some interesting, counter-intuitive relationships between seating capacity and the success of a new worship opportunity. When the church is less than 40 percent full, a new service is *especially* appropriate because the current service is unlikely to grow and unlikely to be impacted negatively by the new one. Adding a service is a touchier matter in a church whose attendance has remained plateaued for several years at 60 to 80 percent of seating capacity, because the new service under those conditions may well draw off some of the current service's strength. Even so, says Arn, starting a new worship opportunity still creates the greatest likelihood of an overall increase in attendance. If a church is actually filled up already (80 to 100 percent of capacity), he recommends the immediate creation of an *identical* service, rather than one of a somewhat different style.

Why Try Something Different?

Arn has identified several strong reasons for expanding the worship opportunities and the range of worship styles. First on the list is the impact on those who are not currently worshipping anywhere. The creation of a new service helps a congregation focus its attention on those who are not here yet, and it challenges leaders to convey the core message in fresh ways. The new service makes it easier for people to invite friends and neighbors. This last point is worth emphasizing. People often hesitate to invite because they don't have confidence that their church's familiar patterns will connect with others; when a meaningful new opportunity is planned, the number of invitations increases dramatically.

The increased variety of times and styles will also minister better to the range of people who are already on our church rolls—active and inactive. The broader culture today fosters in people the expectation that they will have choices in their religious involvement right along with other aspects of their lives. Offering another major worship opportunity, at a different time and in a somewhat different style, guarantees that more kinds of people can participate in our church life without disrupting the patterns that have proven meaningful for many current members. A blended approach (older and newer elements in the same service) often ends up frustrating everyone and undermining the financial stability of the congregation in the process.

What Is a "Somewhat Different" Style?

One of Arn's most helpful contributions to the conversation about multiple worship services is his diagram of the different population groups a given service might be addressing. He incorporates three variables into his scheme. First, he speaks of three generational groupings: seniors (born before 1940), baby boomers (those now arriving at middle age), and the baby bust generation (born after 1965). Second, in relation to faith participation, he distinguishes between believers and seekers. And on the third dimension of social and ethnic identity, he conceives that worship can be oriented toward people of the same culture, people of multiple cultures, or people of a different culture than the dominant group in the congregation. These different possibilities are represented in chart form:

Different Ways Worship Services Can Be Focused

Senior Generation	Baby Boom Generation	Baby Bust Generation
Believer-Focused		Seeker-Focused
Identi-Cultural	Multi-Cultural	Cross-Cultural

Theoretically, there are 18 unique approaches to worship that could be fashioned by choosing one emphasis from each row. But current church life is not nearly that diverse. Arn found that an astounding 96 percent of existing services are designed for people closer to the left-hand side of the chart—believers from the senior or boomer generations who share the same cultural background as existing members. Whether you intend it or not, your church's worship is currently shaped to meet the needs and expectations of some groups more than others.

To plan a new service which will increase your church's total attendance, Arn recommends that you move to *one* adjacent box on only *one* row. One change in one variable will be significant enough to attract an entirely new group of people. Changing more than one variable will make the process of researching and planning the new service not just twice as complicated, but four times so. Changing all three variables to define a new service will require a Herculean effort and reduce the chances of success dramatically.[3]

So, the 96 percent of churches on the left side of the chart will set themselves up for failure if they try, in one jump, to reach non-believer young adults of a different socioeconomic group. Instead, each church can ponder its vocation and gifts (in relation to the community context) and determine just one dimension of learning and change that it will attempt in the next few years. Believer seniors may decide to reach out to seeker seniors instead of looking for young families. A multi-cultural congregation of boomers may focus only on providing a worship option for culturally similar neighbors and offspring in their early twenties.

There is an appealing modesty in this approach. Once we get over the illusion that our church is actually reaching everybody, we can take one clear step toward becoming more inclusive. The modest one-box move is still a demanding goal, requiring deep commitment and perseverance on the part of leaders and members. A church that succeeds in serving one additional subgroup in the population through a sustainable new worship service is much more likely, I believe, to take additional missionary risks in the future.

A Look at the Costs

In order to explore the promising possibility of an additional service, clergy and elected leaders will have to confront their own significant fears, as well as those of the current members. One denomination[4] discovered that pastors and boards were apprehensive about many of the same things, including:

- Physical demands on the clergy
- Loss of unity due to separate congregations; not knowing everyone
- Psychological let-down due to diminishment of the existing service
- Conflict, decreased morale, or a drop in overall attendance

In addition to these common themes, the clergy had substantial fears about the failure of the new project (lack of cooperation or low attendance), while boards were anxious about trying something new and different. The news was good, however, from congregations that actually implemented a new service; respondents to the study all reported that their churches "now felt positive toward the new service, and that it was worth the time, money, and risk involved."[5]

Although those positive results are encouraging, we shouldn't assume that the risk ends when the new service begins to succeed. Pastors will be subject to criticism whether the new service succeeds or not. Arn found that there are three periods when the risk to the pastor peaks: (1) the period between first public airing of the idea and a formal vote; (2) the first three months of the new service; and (3) the 8- to 12- month period after attendance at the new service exceeds attendance at previously existing services.

The first two periods of high risk seem predictable enough, but the third may take leaders by surprise. What we see there is the risk of success:

> In churches that have had only one service or style for ten years or more, the success of the new service may cause greater consternation among many members than would its failure. If the service is successful, the pastor's risk is in the reaction from those who have sanctified the status quo.[6]

Clergy will be ill-equipped to face this kind of risk without a healthy network of emotional support. They will need spiritual guidance from a reliable person or group outside their work setting (which includes both the congregation and the denominational hierarchy) and even some perspective on how they would support themselves financially if they were to leave this particular position.[7]

Arn found that clergy tenure is also a significant factor in determining the costliness of this initiative. During the first year or two, a pastor may succeed in launching a new service as his or her first major project because of the "honeymoon" phenomenon. (The family size church may be an exception here.) In the third through fifth years, the willingness of the congregation to follow a pastor's change initiative drops drastically, so that success will probably require "extraordinary support among established lay leaders," assurance of the pastor's commitment to stay long enough to get the service established, and a few respected leaders who will stand with the pastor when the going gets tough. Once a pastor enters the sixth year and intends to stay a while, members become more and more likely to accept change initiatives.

Pastors need to be prepared for an increased work load, not just to implement the additional service, but also to plan for it week by week and to organize the additional volunteer ministries that will support it. If the vision for the service involves reaching out with a moderately different style to an additional population, Arn suggests that the new service may require four times as much planning time as the current one—placing most of the attention not on development of a different sermon, but on preparation for the whole worship experience with a team of leaders, mostly gifted volunteers.

Critical Mass

The worst way to launch a new worship service is to start small and hope it will grow. It is perfectly normal for a new service to decline 20 to 50 percent during the first few months after it is inaugurated, and you should plan to start big enough to ensure that attendance does not drop below "critical mass" at any time during that period. Arn provides criteria for determining critical mass:

Attendance Goal #1: At least 50 people or 35% of the largest present service (whichever is greater) in attendance. . . . Most new services that begin with less than 50 don't survive the first year. . . .

Attendance Goal #2: At least 35% of those in attendance should be unchurched. . . .Churches generally find that if their new service is focused on a new target group, and adequate promotion to the target audience has occurred, then 65% or more of those in attendance will be unchurched or inactives. . .

Room Capacity Goal: The meeting room should be filled to at least 50% capacity. . . . It may be better to meet in a facility other than the sanctuary.[8]

Critical mass is the "number of people needed to allow the service to continue to grow beyond the first six months." If a new service "begins below, or drops below, the critical mass in the first six months, there is often insufficient energy to begin growing again, and the service will probably die."[9]

Arn's research makes it clear that starting a new service is a challenge. But it is reassuring to know that a well-planned expansion of worship opportunities can help move a stuck congregation off an attendance plateau and even reverse the trend in a declining church.

Biblical Reflection

In the eleventh chapter of Numbers, we see an example of the faith community wanting to enforce uniformity of religious experience. Eldad and Medad are not with the 70 elders gathered around the tent of meeting (their official place of communion with God); instead they are having a profound encounter with the Spirit back in the camp.

1. Read Numbers 11:24-30. Why do you think Joshua wanted Moses to stop Eldad and Medad from expressing the Spirit of God in the camp?

2. What new demands does a congregation experience when everyone does not gather at the same hour for worship?

3. What enrichment of religious expression might be possible for your church through an additional service?

4. Relate this discussion to the final question in the Biblical Reflection section of chapter 4: Can an additional service create a bridge with some group of people God is trying to reach?

Application Exercise

1. Prepare a seating chart for your church showing the number of people that can be accommodated comfortably (30 to 36 inches of space per person).

2. Prepare a parking chart showing how many cars can be accommodated at your main worship service. Ten minutes before each service starts, how many convenient spaces are visible to a first-time visitor?

3. For each of your services, chart the following information. The final column refers to Charles Arn's categories on page 48.

	Average attendance	Percentage of seating capacity utilized	Who this service is designed to reach (age group, believers/ seekers, cultural group)
Service A			
Service B			
Service C			

4. Review the first section of this chapter. To what extent is your church a good candidate for adding a new worship opportunity?

5. Unless your main service is already 80 percent full, Arn recommends that you create a new service of a somewhat different style using the "one-box rule" to define the change. For whom might a new service be designed?

CHAPTER 7

Should We Add Staff?

Staffing Debates at St. Peter's

Let's look again at the attendance chart for the church that I have named St. Peter's. This case provides a clear example of the relationship between staffing decisions and size. (It also illustrates elements of Arn's argument about expanding the number of worship opportunities.)

St. Peter's is an Episcopal church, located in a northeast coastal town dubbed Seaside for our purposes. Although an older Episcopal church lies nestled among the narrow streets of the historic district, St. Peter's is located on the main road running due west out of the town center and stands near the boundary with an adjacent town. The entire area began growing briskly during the 1950s, and St. Peter's was well situated to attract families who were moving into new housing developments. The parish was offering one major worship service (with church school for children at the same hour), plus a quieter, early morning chapel service.

As on the previous chart, I have shown on the horizontal axis the tenures of the two most recent clergy so that the narrative is easier to follow.

Average Attendance
St. Peter's, Seaside

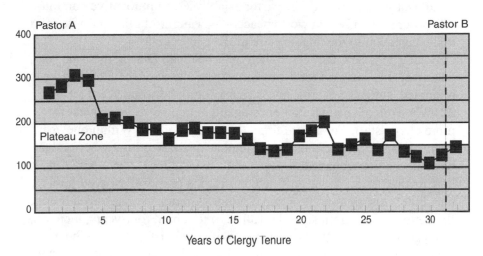

Years of Clergy Tenure

Thirty-two years ago, a new rector (as the primary pastor is called) arrived. Having noted that worship seating and church school space were in short supply, he decided early on to launch an additional Sunday service, complete with its own church school program. Total attendance jumped during his second and third years. Toward the end of the third year, he requested that the vestry (church board) approve a new position for an assistant minister, but this request was denied.

Attendance sagged slightly in the rector's fourth year, then dropped markedly in the fifth—down almost to the 200 level. At that point, he restated the need for additional clergy staff, but was again turned down. Since attendance had declined considerably from its peak above 300, a series of changes ensued over time:

Year 6:   Reduce to one church school opportunity each Sunday
Year 7:   Eliminate part-time church school director
Year 8:   Conduct third worship service during peak attendance period only (September to December)
Year 9:   Renovate sanctuary and improve organ
Year 10: Close church entirely in July
Year 11: Provide training for lay pastoral visitors
Year 13: Eliminate third worship service entirely
Year 15: Offer church school only on alternate weeks

For a total of 11 years, the church bounced up and down within the pastoral-to-program plateau zone (150 to 200), with a general downward trend. During this period, the pastor established an innovative community program focused on world peace—a meaningful ministry with minimal connection to the ongoing life of the congregation.

After 18 years, the rector went on sabbatical. During the time he was away, his energies for the congregation's growth seem to have been rekindled, since the chart shows a sharp upturn between years 19 and 22. When attendance hit 200 once again, he repeated the request for more clergy staff. For a third time, the vestry said no. Within one year, attendance sank to the bottom of the plateau zone—about where it had been before the sabbatical.

As discussion about staffing continued, a proposal evolved for a part-time, confirmation program director. Attendance zigzagged around the bottom of program size (the 150 line) for about four years, then sank into pastoral size for the last few years of his ministry. During the interim after his departure, the vestry asked for help looking at growth issues. Members began preparing the chart and sorted back through vestry minutes to discover what was going on at various stages of their history.

Though some had served as leaders during most of the rector's long tenure, they were stunned to see the effect of the parish's reluctance to add staff. One member commented that the decisions were rooted in the basic fiscal conservatism of the region. Another said that employing an assistant for the rector seemed more like a "perk" than an essential parish resource. Most agreed that the congregation was deeply ambivalent about growing.

The two final data points on the chart represent the church's start-up period with an able and energetic new rector. The vestry seems to be conscious that the whole pattern could repeat itself as attendance builds again in response to new clergy initiatives, but it remains to be seen whether St. Peter's can press through the transition zone and establish itself solidly as a program size church.

Staffing for Growth

Growing churches face a dilemma. They don't have enough households to fully support a new staff person, but they will never gain those households without additional staff energy. In general, a church must staff somewhat ahead of the immediate need in order to keep growing. St. Peter's kept lagging behind the immediate need and so precipitated a decline.

Roy Oswald's article in the appendix provides a guideline: "As a rule of thumb, if you desire to staff for growth, you need one full-time program person on your staff for every one hundred active members [usually based on average attendance]. . . . You are staffing for maintenance if you are just slightly under that figure. You are staffed for decline if you are seriously under that figure." This one-per-hundred rule assumes that you already have the basic services of a church musician (worship planning, Sunday music leadership, a midweek rehearsal); staffing for growth might involve adding hours or personnel to start additional choirs, plan a new kind of service, or link music with community outreach. Secretarial support and janitorial staff are also needed over and above the one-per-hundred mark.

The St. Peter's case fits this guideline well. With a full-time pastor and a part-time church school director, they were staffed to grow through the 150 level—and they did. As soon as they added a worship service and a church school session (excellent moves to meet the opportunity at their doorstep), they fell into a severe staff deficit. Failure to address the problem plunged St. Peter's into decline and they shrank back down toward the 150 mark. Eliminating the church school director exacerbated the downward slide, which was only partially mitigated by intensifying lay ministries. (Important in themselves, excellent lay ministries require additional staff support and oversight.) The tide didn't turn in a positive direction until the church school staff position was restored. St. Peter's needs the equivalent of two full-time program staff if it wants to break out of the plateau zone (150 to 200) and stabilize as a program size church.

Typical Patterns

Carl George offers some staffing scenarios,[1] which I have adapted to fit the size and plateau zone terminology used in this book. "Full-time" and "part-time" are abbreviated (FT and PT) and refer to position "equivalents"; some churches prefer to involve two different people in the equivalent of one position. Remember that significant volunteer leadership is essential, in addition to paid staff positions.

Staffing for Growth

Pastoral size	FT pastor + basic services of church musician + PT secretary + basic janitorial services
	⇩
	Add PT minister of education
	⇩
	Increase secretary to FT
	⇩
Plateau zone	FT senior pastor + FT minister of education + PT minister of youth + expanded PT music ministry + FT secretary + PT custodian
	⇩
Program size	FT senior pastor + FT minister of education + FT minister of youth + extended music ministry + FT and PT secretary + FT custodian + intern
	⇩
Plateau zone	FT senior pastor + FT minister of education + FT minister of youth + FT minister of music + 2 FT secretaries + FT and PT custodian + intern
	⇩
Corporate size	Above pattern + specialty associate ministers for life-stage divisions
	⇩
	Add FT business manager

"Life-stage divisions" included in the corporate size scenario are high-quality, multi-faceted ministries with children, collegians, young adults, or senior adults. Some denominations find this "divisional" way of thinking quite unfamiliar, but according to George, such an approach creates vital sub-congregations which can meet targeted spiritual needs and effectively draw others from the same life stage.

Funding New Staff

Without a doubt, adding staff involves risk. But I hope the St. Peter's case has proved to you that refusing to add staff can be an even bigger risk when growth opportunities are present in the community and potential members are standing on your doorstep. The trick is to come up with a financial strategy to stay slightly ahead of your growth curve. Here is the assessment of church growth leader Bill Sullivan:

> If the increased staff is properly deployed and supervised, they will pay for themselves. At the time of hiring, you probably need only half the necessary money [for the first year]. . . . Their ministry should bring in [the rest]. . . . I always expected a staff person to pull about 10 couples around himself, 2 or 3 of these being families already in the church. . . . That's fine. But beyond those I expected them to pull about 6 or 7 other couples out of our prospect list. . . . [W]e are not talking about multiplying staff as an ecclesiastical status symbol. . . . And we are certainly not talking about creating staff so the pastor doesn't have to work as hard. . . .[2]

Sullivan cautions against seeing new staff members as "assisting" the senior pastor with the same tasks he or she already does, or as picking up what he or she doesn't want to do. New staff should extend the reach of the congregation into new areas (geographic, demographic, programmatic) and multiply ministry many times over through the members they will equip.

The plan for financing an additional program staff position should point to the populations and opportunities which that position is supposed to reach. As the St. Peter's case makes clear, staffing, space (including parking), and an expanded worship schedule need to be woven together into a coherent pattern in light of parish strengths and community demographics.

Biblical Reflection

Soon after the people of Israel had left Egypt, Moses encountered a personal crisis: He had slipped into the assumption that he personally had to solve all problems and fill all needs. Since Moses' family could see clearly what this style of ministry was doing to him, Jethro took him aside and suggested that he "expand his staff."

1. Read Exodus 18:13-23. Imagine what Zipporah (Moses' wife) might have been saying to Jethro just before verse 14.

2. How would you have responded to Jethro's advice? What prevents you from delegating parts of a task to other leaders?

3. What specific ministries in your church are unnecessarily limited or burdensome because they now fall on only one person?

4. What advice do you imagine Jethro might have for your congregation regarding its staffing pattern?

Application Exercise

1. Assess whether your church is staffed for growth, plateau, or decline. Use the following methods:

   a. Use the one-per-hundred rule (page 57):
      Average attendance ÷ 100 = Number of program staff needed for growth (in addition to basic services of a church musician)

      Our average attendance: _____ ÷ 100 = _____
                                                   (full-time equivalents)

      Our current number of program staff = _____
      (in addition to basic music)   *(full-time equivalents)*

b. Refer to the section titled Typical Patterns (page 58). Which staffing configuration comes closest to your own? How does your staff pattern match up with the recommended size (headings at left of the chart)?

2. If you are understaffed for the growth to which you aspire, what new or expanded positions might have the greatest priority?

CHAPTER 8

What Will It Take to Make the Change?

Adaptive Work

Size change raises fundamental questions of identity and purpose which require more than a technical response. Psychiatrist and educator Ronald Heifetz[1] calls these deeper challenges "adaptive work." Technical work in the congregation—what happens when we call the electrician because the lights won't come on—requires little learning on our part as members. The expert finds the problem, defines the solution, and does the work. All we have to do is flick the light switch and pay the bill. An adaptive challenge, on the other hand, requires real learning and change on the part of the congregation itself, in some or all phases of the work: defining the central issues, deciding on a response, and implementing the decisions. The weight of responsibility for working on the problem shifts dramatically from the technical expert to the church's own leaders and members.

In biblical terms we might contrast the exodus with the journey in the wilderness. One could say that crossing the sea on dry land was essentially technical work. God empowered Moses with sufficient expertise to name the injustice, direct the departure from Egypt, and remove the obstacles. The people were not required to do much more than walk. But at the moment they left the chariots behind in the mud, 40 years of adaptive work began. Those who had been "no people" had to take on a weighty new identity as "God's people." Slaves who had always been governed by Pharaoh had to learn how to organize themselves. The faith community which received the law at Sinai had to establish different patterns of life—a new culture—which would embody the divine purposes revealed to them. So profound was the required transformation that no one who remembered Egypt could enter the land of promise.

In the face of a size transition, pastors, boards, and program heads are called on to provide a type of leadership that may be unfamiliar to them and unexpected in the congregation. As if shifting their weight from one foot to the other, leaders will need to decrease their emphasis on giving answers and maintaining order while increasing their emphasis on the learning required by a new situation. Heifetz calls attention to five shifts in leadership focus that can help a system to meet an adaptive challenge.

First, church leaders who discern an adaptive challenge will be more effective if they resist the expectation (from others and from within themselves) that they will take total responsibility for both understanding the problem and developing the solution while others in the system continue with business as usual. Instead, these leaders will shift their energies toward alerting the congregation that there is uncharted territory ahead and preparing people for an "off-road" adventure. Leadership will consist mostly of asking unexpected, even subversive, questions about what is happening in the congregation and its environment.

Second, effective leaders will not move too quickly to reassure people in the face of an adaptive challenge. Pastors and boards often want to tell nervous members that numerical growth won't affect the character of the church, but people know instinctively that growth means change. In order to develop an appropriate sense of urgency and motivation, the congregation needs to see the potential threats before them. The members themselves need to help calculate the cost of making— and of avoiding—a size transition.

Third, leaders confronting an adaptive challenge will not reinforce expected roles. Rather, they will encourage curiosity about the way roles are shifting and ask people to interact in novel ways as learning occurs. When exploring a possible size transition, it helps to cut across the boxes and lines on the church's organizational chart, fostering conversation among people who don't ordinarily talk to each other or make decisions together.

Fourth, leaders in a size transition will resist pressure to stuff the genie back in the bottle and restore immediate order. Rather, they will notice, explore, and make visible the "rubs" that are occurring so that the energy generated by those conflicts can help power the congregation's learning.

Finally, leaders of adaptive work will allow the norms (unwritten rules) of the congregation to be examined and challenged. As the "threat" of growth becomes apparent to members, and some of them demand that leaders defend the status quo, it takes courage to stand for open exploration. Roy Oswald's workbook *Making Your Church More Inviting*[2] outlines steps for examining congregational norms, especially through the eyes of the newest members.

A Holding Environment

Central to Heifetz's view of leadership is the conviction that people with positional authority can create a holding environment for adaptive work. This is the organizational equivalent of a pressure cooker—an adjustable vessel strong enough to contain dramatic, even violent, transformative processes during the period of time needed for a new synthesis to occur. Pursuing this analogy, Heifetz urges official leadership to "keep the heat up without blowing up the vessel" by giving the work of adaptation "back to the people, but at a rate they can stand" and by offering some protection to people at the edge of the organization who "point to the internal contradictions" in the system.[3]

In a size transition, one element of the holding environment may be a definite period of structured, congregation-wide study. The pastor and board would develop and publish clear steps for the study process; they would specify how different parts of the system would be involved (including some unconventional groupings); and they would indicate procedures by which decisions would ultimately be made. Engaging a skilled third party to facilitate the study process could further strengthen the container. Outsiders who are perceived as fair and impartial can help official leaders modulate the pressure by allowing members to blow off a little steam or by holding their feet to the fire when the central questions are being avoided.

Spiritual and Institutional Urgency

Studying transformation efforts in business organizations, John Kotter[4] has observed that over half of these major change projects fail due to an inadequate sense of urgency. In the successful cases, someone has looked hard at key facts and trends, discerned an approaching crisis or a great opportunity, and provided a dramatic picture of these findings that could galvanize attention throughout the system. The implications of Kotter's work for the in-between church are clear: Until three-quarters of your formal and informal leadership cadre is "honestly convinced that business-as-usual is totally unacceptable,"[5] your church's concerted effort to change sizes is not ready to be launched.

Organizational theorists Danny Miller and Peter Friesen[6] have highlighted in their work the value of some delay in changing from one organizational configuration to another, precisely because so much motivation is required to make the shift. Throughout the system, leaders must feel in their bones that the cost of "staying where we are" outweighs the risk of reconfiguring, and this sense of urgency does not develop without time and persistent leadership effort. The organizations they judged to be successful in completing major transitions were found to "minimize the number of change periods, and move through the periods as quickly as possible."[7] During most eras of their history, these entities maintained enormous stability and made few changes; occasionally, they geared up for swift and dramatic transformation. Church leaders frequently violate both parts of this prescription by keeping members constantly off-balance with piecemeal changes, and also by failing to mobilize the whole system for a decisive move when major threats or opportunities knock at the door. (Think about the St. Peter's case in this regard.)

Look back over your own congregation's size history and ask yourself these questions: What was the perceived urgency that moved your congregation through growth plateaus in the past? How did leaders communicate that urgency? How well have you dramatized the cost of staying where you are for your whole leadership group? What smaller adjustments might you forgo while you are getting the congregation ready for a change on many dimensions at once?

For religious leaders, building the sense of urgency for change in size is not simply an institutional matter. The term "corporate," now

associated mostly with big business, is derived from the Latin word
corpus. The congregation's corporate vocation is the issue here—the
vocation of the Body. Only a clear sense of God's call can draw us
beyond our myriad anxieties toward a purpose compelling enough to
engender risk and sacrifice. Provocative questions about the congregation's reason for being may arise anywhere in the system: from a pastor,
a core leader, a new member, a wise old man or woman, or someone
standing at the very fringe of church life. But those with positions of
formal authority—especially the pastor and the board—are responsible
for shaping an environment in which prayer and conversation about the
church's deepest purpose can be sustained until clarity begins to emerge.

In a multi-cultural, multi-faith society, many mainstream congregations lose their nerve when they try to articulate a spiritual basis for
reaching out to others. In part, this silence may arise from a valid reluctance to intrude or impose. But muteness about the urgency of in-
vitational ministry often arises from a malnourished congregational
spirituality—weakness in fostering faith practices that help people enter
into and interpret a firsthand encounter with God. Sociologists of reli-
gion Kirk Hadaway and David Roozen put it this way:

> Mainstream churches deaden religious experience among their
> members because they give it no visible expression. They rela-
> tivize it; they rationalize it; they bury it in rote tradition. . . . The
> growing [mainline] congregations are the spiritually oriented . . .
> churches. Such churches are unapologetically liberal and heavily
> involved in community ministry, with a clear focus on social
> justice. Yet the social and moral agenda of these churches is
> anchored in a deep, meaningful worship experience [which
> conveys] the expectation, the presumption, the surety that God
> is present in the service and in the lives of anyone who is open
> to God's Spirit.[8]

Across denominations, more and more resources are available for
recovering and deepening the spiritual life of congregations. Rekindling
people's desire for God is right at the heart of the matter.

Powerful Partnership between Clergy and Lay Leaders

Kotter speaks of the need for a powerful "guiding coalition"[9] to head up a transformation process. You will notice that he is speaking like a community organizer here ("building a coalition") rather than using more conventional management or governance terms. For dramatic change to occur, a top positional leader (senior pastor or chief elected officer) needs to assemble an ad hoc team of people whose combined influence—based on the position, knowledge, and respect they have in the congregation—is sufficient to get big things done.

This guiding coalition will never include the whole church board because people are so frequently elected to fulfill what Kotter calls a "management mandate . . . to minimize risk and keep the current system operating."[10] It may, on the other hand, include a new member with the right skills; an unexpected staff person, like the church musician or the nursery school director; former elected officers who see the problem; younger leaders who will soon be stepping up into top elected and appointed positions; and perhaps a skilled person from the denominational office who is willing to partner with congregations preparing themselves for change. The guiding coalition should only include people who have a problem-solving attitude and work well with others. It must involve a number of those who currently provide primary leadership in significant church programs, groups, or ministries (not just rotating committee members with little direct responsibility for the action).

Where does the pastor fit in? Sometimes clergy are the first to recognize the need for size transition because they are caught in the daily crunch of conflicting expectations. Kotter notes how many business transformations begin well because of a "new head who is a good leader and . . . sees the need for a major change."[11] This pattern was visible in the case of St. Peter's. Clergy are not always trained or expected, however, to lead dramatic change in church systems. If another top leader has the organizational skills, it may be sufficient for the pastor to act as a partner and offer solid spiritual foundation to the effort. In the smallest churches (under 25 or so in attendance) or in congregations seeking to relinquish the ghost of pastoral size structures in favor of their family size reality, the guiding coalition may consist only of lay persons. Ideally, this group will team up with denominational or parachurch resource people who can help them envision vital, sustainable patterns of home-grown ministry.

Though it may be relatively easy to recruit this guiding coalition, someone still has to take responsibility for helping them become a committed team. In business the group may participate in a series of off-site retreats spread over a period of months. Churches frequently bring in a consultant to work first with the wider leadership corps—providing common language about size transition—and then with a smaller "transition planning task force" (guiding coalition) of six to nine persons, including the senior pastor.

Tolerance for Unhappiness

Many congregations live in "the happiness trap." Gil Rendle, a senior consultant at the Alban Institute, describes this common church dynamic:

> Often, congregational leaders want to "fix" their congregation, meaning correcting complaints and making it "perfect" for everyone. Instead, I suggest a healthier response: to work toward faithfulness rather than happiness. I advise them to go back to their mission statement or their understanding of their congregation's call to ministry and develop decisions that support such a position.[12]

Paradoxically, when leaders try to fix everything they hear complaints about, they actually stimulate new objections from the opposite direction. This is natural, because living systems have powerful (if subtle) ways of maintaining equilibrium. Change any part, and the rest of the system is sure to react.

So what's the alternative? Instead of trying to keep everybody happy, clergy and lay leaders would do better to see themselves "managing differences."[13] In a size transition, some people will be attracted to the kind of organizational analysis laid out in this book, while others will find it totally irrelevant to their sense of what is right for their church. Some members have never experienced a well-functioning congregation of the next size and can't imagine the satisfactions it might provide, yet others are missing those benefits rather acutely. Some congregants have a great deal of resilience in times of transition, while others experience change as trauma.

One important set of differences is delineated by the pastor's age and tenure.[14] Those congregants who are both younger and newer than the pastor will look to this person for direction. Those older and longer tenured than the pastor will expect him or her to follow their lead.

Differences in Political Alignment of Members

	Older than Pastor	Younger than Pastor
Newer than pastor	*AREAS OF POTENTIAL POLARIZATION*	See pastor as leader or commander
Predate pastor	See pastor as chaplain or hired hand	

The diagonal line defines an area of potential polarization. Some older newcomers and younger, long-time members will tend to follow the pastor in a major initiative, while others from the same groupings will tend to side with church elders (well-established lay leadership).

This chart makes it clearer why the family-to-pastoral size transition occurs most readily when the pastor has stayed a very long time: In a system which integrates newcomers very slowly, it takes many years for the pastor to gain sufficient political stature to be acknowledged as the congregation's central leader. It also helps illuminate the mourning and depression that churches experience when the central role of pastor must be relinquished in favor of family size structures. Those who were drawn to the congregation during the ministry of the last full-time pastor (especially if this was a long tenure) are unlikely to see any advantage in an innovative ministry approach that develops lay pastors, preachers, teachers, and administrators from within the congregation. In any of the

possible size transitions, however, analyzing leadership expectations will
help the guiding coalition to manage differences.

Purpose and Plan

Once the guiding coalition becomes convinced that a dramatic change is
needed, there is still major work to do. Fundraisers tell us that people do
not contribute money to problems, no matter how dire. They contribute
to solutions, the practical steps toward an overarching purpose that they
deeply embrace. The leadership team will need to develop a plan that is
both spiritually compelling and sensible. The following sections describe
some elements of that plan.

The "Why" of Size Transition

*Show dramatically who and what is being lost because of the way you
do things now.* In the Alban Institute's research on new member incorporation,[15] church boards were powerfully impressed by the information
that was gathered from newcomers and visitors, including some who had
decided not to continue coming. Most church leaders want to see themselves as hospitable and inclusive, but cannot imagine clearly what outsiders may be experiencing as they try to make a connection. They need
to see what the overall patterns are; a single example is not enough to
persuade people that pervasive change is needed. Members of the guiding coalition should reflect back on their own process of decision making
and ask: What five facts were most influential in convincing me that a
size change is needed? Those facts need to be woven into a story that
can be told in five minutes, with bold visual aids provided to reinforce
the message.

The "What" of Size Transition

*Help people peer over the imaginary threshold into a future rich with
spiritual and personal meaning.* The Hebrew slaves were compelled
to leave Egypt by an image of release from oppression. Once they had

launched out into the wilderness, that vision had to be fleshed out. Increasingly, they were drawn forward by the picture of a land flowing with milk and honey, promising them a dignity they had never before experienced. Once they were nobodies, but soon they would be God's chosen nation with a place in both world geography and world history.

Although a phrase like "pastoral-to-program transition" is helpful shorthand for those who already believe a change is right and good, it will hardly compel the hearts of people who are devoted to your congregation and its familiar practices. The vision story needs to sound more like this:

> Last week, I made six pastoral visits to newcomers, the sick, the homebound. But here is a list of 60 people who would have been deeply touched by a personal contact from our church. Here is a another list of a dozen people in their twenties who don't know each other and don't attend much. And here is a list of 50 active seniors who could help each other with life issues much better than I can. In the course of a single week, this church could reach out to all these people—not just six—if we stop thinking that I'm the only minister.

I have put this statement into the pastor's voice as an illustration of what vision-talk sounds like. But the guiding coalition needs to develop a voice of its own and be able to describe in a compelling way how this church might live out its purpose. This story too must be honed down to a coherent five-minute presentation which any member of the guiding coalition can share at the drop of a hat. Kotter says your guiding coalition isn't ready to engage others in the system until this powerful story is discovered.[16]

The "Who" of Size Transition

Assess what groups you are reaching with current programs and ministries, then focus on expanding to reach one box at a time (chapter 6). Your pin map from chapter 4 will give you some clues about the expansion of ministry in this transition. If you used a special color for those who have started coming most recently, you can do some analysis

of your church's current power to draw people. Are those newest households from a younger generation? Are they less familiar with the Bible
or worship practices? Are they uncertain about what they believe and
hesitant to sign on for baptism or confirmation? Do they live in a different area than those who joined 20 years ago? Although some of your
newest members may match the previous ones rather closely, you may
find that you are gaining a toehold in a new population group. A decision to focus more carefully on that group might be one way to launch
your transition solidly through the plateau.

Size transitions often fail to occur because the congregation doesn't
ever reach critical mass of a new population group. You may have a
steady stream of visitors from the twenty-something generation, but each
time a single adult or young family comes in, they see few others like
themselves. Getting a better foothold with that group may require financial investment in a part-time staff person with demonstrated ability
to reach that group, plus one high-quality, new program tailored just for
them.

The "How" of Size Transition

Spell out practical steps that everyone can understand. Although each
of the six possible transitions (see chapter 3) has a different focus, goals
like these might be included:

1. *Strengthen new member incorporation structures and practices.*
Improve the quality with which you invite, greet, orient, and incorporate
people, then send them into daily life with a faith-based sense of purpose.[17]

2. *Multiply ministries by shifting expectations and structures for
pastoral care.* Help pastor and congregation shift to roles in which
clergy take more responsibility to recruit, train, and support lay pastoral care teams.

3. *Establish a significant pattern of small group ministry.* In these
groups people relate their faith to daily life. To make a difference, the
pattern has to be widespread in the congregation, not just an add-on for

the few. Multiplication can occur if every group has an apprentice leader who can continue with the established group when the more experienced leader moves off to form a new one.[18]

4. *Start an additional worship service.* Unless your seating is already 80 to 100 percent full on an average Sunday, consider making the new service a somewhat different style.

5. *Increase church staff.* Use the guidelines discussed in chapter 7 to create a pattern that allows for natural growth.

These goals need to fit together into a coherent pattern so that mutually reinforcing elements can be put in place at the same time.

The "Time Frame" of Size Transition

Set a goal and break through in bursts of intense effort. Someone told me recently about the way Sweden changed its whole traffic system from "drive on the left" to "drive on the right." All the new traffic signs were painted and put in place with covers over them. Drivers were alerted for months in advance that the change was coming. Then, at noon on one appointed day, every car in Sweden stopped and moved to the other side of the road. With so many complex driving interactions to contend with, the only alternative to bedlam was a swift, all-at-once change. The Swedes pulled it off.

Size transition requires a bit of that all-at-once quality—it is by far the kindest way, as well as the most effective, to accomplish the goal. Set a three-year goal *well beyond the transition zone*, since some falling back is predictable before the new size takes hold. Then launch each stage of your transition with energy. In order to draw the critical mass of attendees, you might make use of strategies such as "Invite-a-Friend Sunday" or a dramatic "opening" of your redesigned church school. You might organize a blitz of visitation to inactive members, visitors, and prospective members. Some congregations have good success reaching children with a church bus route.[19]

It will probably take more than one push and more than one strategy to get enough people assembled in three years so that energy starts to generate itself. During that time you will need to be creative about space and schedule. Churches that wait until they can afford a bigger building will probably never get there.

Biblical Reflection

When the people of Israel left Sinai to begin their 40 years of transition, they did not go alone. God showed them a way to take the "holy ground" of Sinai with them wherever they went. The ark of the covenant became the receptacle for their "portable treasures of faith." Before you conclude your study of size transition, assemble the portable treasures that symbolize for your congregation the promise of God's presence, no matter where the journey may take you.

1. Read Exodus 25:10-22. If this is a group study, bring into the room a large, decorated cardboard box to symbolize the ark.

2. Identify the portable treasures of faith that your congregation has been given by God—the beliefs, practices, and values that you can carry with you into any future situation and still express your deepest identity as God's people. In a group setting, give people craft supplies and ask each to create a symbol of one portable treasure that seems absolutely essential for the journey ahead.

3. In a period of worship to conclude your group study, ask each person to describe his or her symbol, thank God for the gift it represents, and place it in the ark. Appoint one or two scribes for this ceremony who will write down what each person says about the symbol. Create a special place where the box will remain during the time the congregation is discerning God's call with respect to size and creating a plan for action. Go back to the symbols as often as you need to in order to stay in touch with what is truly essential.

4. Draw on the written statements and visual symbols when it comes time to talk with the congregation about size decisions. You might bring members together in clusters of five to ten people (depending on the total number present) to repeat the exercise by discussing

individual proposals and then choosing one treasure which the group will symbolize visually and place in the ark.

Application Exercise

1. Review the section of this chapter entitled Powerful Partnership between Clergy and Lay Leaders. List ten people who would be important members of a guiding coalition.

2. How will you build an adequate sense of urgency throughout the congregation?

3. Based on the discussion in the Purpose and Plan section of this chapter, work with the guiding coalition to draft a written proposal for changing sizes that addresses these key questions:

   a. Why change sizes?
   b. What is our vision for life at another size?
   c. What population groups do we intend to focus on?
   d. How will the transition be accomplished?
   e. What will be our time frame to moving solidly into the next size?

How to Minister Effectively in Family, Pastoral, Program, and Corporate Size Churches

From Chapter 2, Making Your Church More Inviting, *by Roy Oswald (Washington, D.C.: the Alban Institute, 1992).*

The theory of congregational size that I find most workable is Arlin Rothauge's, described in his booklet *Sizing Up a Congregation for New Member Ministry*. It was originally written to help congregations recognize the different ways different-sized churches assimilate new members. When a theory is on target, however, it so accurately reflects reality that it can be applied to other dimensions of a church's life and work. Rothauge's theory elicits consistent "ahas" from clergy who are reflecting on their transition from one size parish to another. Whether churches are growing or downsizing, congregations hold on to deeply ingrained assumptions about what constitutes a dynamic church and what effective clergy do. The inflexibility of these expectations is an important cause of clergy malfunctioning.

Rothauge sets forth four basic congregational sizes. Each size requires a specific cluster of behaviors from its clergy. The average number of people attending weekly worship and the amount of money being contributed regularly provide the most accurate gauge of church size. Since membership rolls fluctuate wildly depending on how frequently they are evaluated, they cannot provide an accurate measurement of congregational size. Rothauge also holds that a church's size category is a matter of attitude as much as numbers. I knew of one congregation that averaged 700 at Sunday worship and still functioned on a Pastoral model. All the pastor did was preach on Sunday and visit people through the week. The pastor's perception of his job burned him out and eventually cost him his marriage and his ministry.

Here is a brief description of each of Rothauge's four sizes and my understanding of what members expect of clergy in each size.

The Patriarchal/Matriarchal Church: Up to Fifty Active Members

This small church can also be called a Family Church because it functions like a family, with appropriate parental figures. The patriarchs and matriarchs control the church's leadership needs. What Family Churches want from clergy is pastoral care, period. For clergy to assume that they are also the chief executive officer and the resident religious authority is to make a serious blunder. The key role of the patriarch or matriarch is to see that clergy do not take the congregation off on a new direction of ministry. Clergy are to be the chaplain of this small family. When clergy don't understand this, they are likely to head into a direct confrontation with the parental figure. It is generally suicide for clergy to get caught in a showdown with the patriarchs and matriarchs within the first five years of their ministry in that place.

Clergy should not assume, however, that they have no role beyond pastoral care. In addition to providing quality worship and home/hospital visitation, clergy can play an important role as consultants to these patriarchs or matriarchs, befriending these parental figures and working alongside them, yet recognizing that when these parental figures decide against an idea, it's finished.

Clergy should watch out for the trap set when members complain to them about the patriarch or matriarch of the parish and encourage the pastor to take the parental figure on. Clergy who respond to such mutinous bids, expecting the congregation to back them in the showdown, betray their misunderstanding of the dynamics of small-church ministry. The high turnover of clergy in these parishes has taught members that in the long run they have to live with old Mr. Schwartz who runs the feed-mill even when they don't like him. Hence it is far too risky for members to get caught siding with pastors who come and go against their resident patriarch/matriarch.

Because these congregations usually cannot pay clergy an acceptable salary, many clergy see them as stepping stones to more rewarding opportunities. It is not unusual for a congregation of this size to list five

successive clergy for every ten years of congregational life. As Lyle
Schaller claims, the longer the pastorates the more powerful clergy become. The shorter the pastorates the more powerful the laity become.
These Family Churches have to develop one or two strong lay leaders at
the center of their life. How else would they manage their ongoing exis-
tence through those long vacancies and through the short pastorates of
the ineffective clergy who are often sent their way?

The president of the Alban Institute, Loren Mead, began his ministry in a Family Church in South Carolina. Later in his ministry he at-
tended a clergy conference at which he discovered seven other clergy
who had also started their ordained ministry in the same parish. As they
talked, those clergy realized that, in view of the difference in their styles
and the shortness of their tenures, the only way that parish survived was
to take none of them seriously.

One of the worst places to go right out of seminary is to a Patriar-
chal/Matriarchal Church. Seminarians are up to their eyeballs in new
theories and good ideas. They want to see if any of them work. Even
though some of those good ideas might be the ticket to their small
church's long-term growth and development, the church's openness to
trying any of them is next to zero. Sometimes, through the sheer force
of personal persuasion, a pastor will talk a congregation into trying a
new program or two. Pretty soon parishioners find themselves coming
to church events much more than they really need to or want to. As they
begin then to withdraw their investment from these new programs, the
clergy inevitably take it personally. Concluding that their gifts for ministry are not really valued in this place, they begin to seek a call else-
where. On the way out of the church they give it a kick, letting the parish know in subtle ways that they are a miserable example of Christian
community.

These small congregations have endured such recriminations for
decades. The message they get from their executive is that they are a
failure because they fail to grow while consuming inordinate amounts
of time. Middle judicatories try to merge them, yoke them, close them
—mostly to no avail. You can't kill these congregations with a stick.
Large churches are far more vulnerable. An exec can place an incompetent pastor in a large church and lose 200 members in one year. Yet the
same exec can throw incompetent clergy at Family Churches, leave
them vacant for years, ignore them—all with little effect. The Family
Church has learned to survive by relying on its own internal leadership.

These congregations need a pastor to stay and love them over at least ten years. This pastor would have to play by the rules and defer to the patriarch's or matriarch's leadership decisions for the first three to five years. At about year four or five, when the pastor did not leave, the congregation might find itself in somewhat of a crisis. At some level they would be saying, "What do you mean you are going to stay? No clergy stay here. There must be something the matter with you." Then the questioning might begin: "Can we really trust you? Naw! You are going to leave us like all the rest." In this questioning we can see the pain of these congregations. For a minute, let's put ourselves in their shoes and imagine an ordained leader walking out on us every few years, berating us on the way out. Would we invest in the next pastor who came to us? Not likely! It would be simply too painful. The Family Church may have invested in one five years ago, only to find that the pastor left just when things started to move. Basically these people have learned not to trust clergy who repeatedly abandon ship when they see no evidence of church growth.

I conclude that we need to refrain from sending these congregations seminary trained pastors. History demonstrates that these churches have not been served well by full-time ordained clergy. The Episcopal Diocese of Nevada and the North Indiana Conference of the United Methodist Church are among judicatories experimenting with employing persons indigenous to the communities, providing them with some basic training to give long-term pastoral care on a part-time basis. I believe long-term tent-making ministries offer the best possibility for ministering to many of these Patriarchal/Matriarchal Churches.

If denominations and middle judicatories persist in placing newly ordained clergy in these parishes, they should do so only after laying out this theory for these clergy, helping them discover who indeed are the patriarchs and matriarchs of the parish, suggesting some strategies for working with them. If these clergy find it simply too difficult to work with these parental figures, they need to let their executive know promptly. Rather than leaving these newly ordained clergy regretting that they pursued ordained ministry in the first place, the exec should move them out of the Family Church.

The Pastoral Church: 50 to 150 Active Members

Clergy are usually at the center of a Pastoral Church. There are so many parental figures around that they need someone at the center to manage them. A leadership circle, made up of the pastor and a small cadre of lay leaders, replaces the patriarchs and matriarchs of the Family Church. The power and effectiveness of the leadership circle depends upon good communication with the congregation and the ability of the pastor to delegate authority, assign responsibility, and recognize the accomplishments of others. Without such skill, the central pastoral function weakens the entire structure. The clergyperson becomes overworked, isolated, and exhausted, may be attacked by other leaders, and finally the harmony of the fellowship circle degenerates.

A key feature of a Pastoral Church is that lay persons experience having their spiritual needs met through their personal relationship with a seminary trained person. In a Pastoral Church it would be rare for a Bible study or a prayer group to meet without the pastor. The pastor is also readily available in times of personal need and crisis. If a parishioner called the pastor and indicated that she needed some personal attention, the pastor would drop over to see her, probably that afternoon but certainly within the week—a qualitatively different experience from being told that the first available appointment to see the pastor in her office is two weeks from now. The time demands on the pastor of a Pastoral Church can become oppressive, however, most members will respond with loyalty to a reasonable level of attention and guidance from this central figure.

A second feature of the Pastoral Church is its sense of itself as a family where everyone knows everyone else. If you show up at church with your daughter Julie by the hand, everyone will greet you and Julie, too. When congregations begin to have 130 to 150 people coming every Sunday morning, they begin to get nervous. As Carl Dudley put it in *Unique Dynamics of the Small Church* (Washington, DC: The Alban Institute, 1977) they begin to feel "stuffed." Members wonder about the new faces they don't know—people who don't know *them*. Are they beginning to lose the intimate fellowship they prize so highly?

Clergy also begin to feel stressed when they have more than 150 active members whom they try to know in depth. In fact, this is one of the reasons why clergy may keep the Pastoral Church from growing to the next larger size congregation—the Program Church. If clergy have the idea firmly fixed in their head that they are ineffective as a pastor unless they can relate in a profound and personal way with every member of the parish, then 150 active members (plus perhaps an even larger number of inactive members) is about all one person can manage.

There are some clergy who function at their highest level of effectiveness in the Pastoral Church. Given the different clusters of skills required for other sizes of congregations, some clergy should consider spending their entire career in this size congregation. Since the Pastoral Church can offer a pastor a decent salary, clergy do tend to stick around longer. If clergy can regard themselves as successful only when they become pastor of a large congregation, then sixty-five percent of mainline Protestant clergy are going to end their careers with feelings of failure. Two-thirds of mainline Protestant congregations are either Family or Pastoral Churches.

Clergy with strong interpersonal skills fare well in the Pastoral Church. These clergy can feed continually on the richness of direct involvement in the highs and lows of people's lives. Clergy who enjoy being at the center of most activities also do well. There are lots of opportunities to preach and lead in worship and to serve as primary instructors in many class settings for both young and old. Outgoing, expressive people seem to be the best matches for the style of ministry in the Pastoral Church. An open, interactive leadership style also seems to suit this size church best.

Growth in the Pastoral Church will depend mainly on the popularity and effectiveness of the pastor. People join the church because they like the interaction between pastor and people. When new people visit the congregation for the first time, it is likely to be the pastor who will make the follow-up house call.

When a congregation grows to the point where its pastor's time and energy is drawn off into many other activities and the one-on-one pastoral relationship begins to suffer, it may hire additional staff to handle these new functions so the pastor can once again have plenty of time for interpersonal caring. Unfortunately, this strategy will have limited success. To begin with, when you hire additional staff you then have a multiple staff, which requires staff meetings, supervision, delegation, evaluation, and planning. These activities draw the pastor deeper into administration. Then, too, additional staff members tend to specialize in such

things as Christian education, youth ministry, evangelism, or stewardship, which tends to add to the administrative role of the head of staff
rather than freeing his or her time up for pastoral care.

Clergy consider a congregation's transition from Pastoral to Program size the most difficult. One can expect enormous resistance on the
part of a Pastoral Church as it flirts with becoming a Program Church.
Many churches make an unconscious choice not to make the transition
and keep hovering around the level of 150 active members. The two
treasured features of a Pastoral Church that will be lost if it becomes a
Program Church are ready access to their religious leaders and the feeling of oneness as a church family, where everyone knows everyone else
and the church can function as a single cell community.

Two things can prevent a congregation from making that transition:
The first barrier is found in the clergy. When clergy hold on to a need to
be connected in depth to all the active members, they become the bot-
tlenecks to growth. The second barrier is found in the lay leaders who
are unwilling to have many of their spiritual needs met by anyone except
their ordained leader.

It is most helpful to put this theory up on newsprint before the chief
decision-making body of the church and ask where it thinks the parish
stands. If they have been saying "yes, yes" to church growth with their
lips, but "no, no" with their behavior, this theory can bring their resistance to the conscious level by pointing out the real costs they will face
in growing. Churches tend to grow when parish leaders, fully aware of
the cost of growth, make a conscious decision to proceed.

Without the backing of key lay leaders, the cost of moving from a
Pastoral to a Program Church usually comes out of the pastor's hide.
The parish may welcome the pastor's efforts in parish program development, while still expecting all the parish calling and one-on-one work to
continue at the same high level as before. Burnout and/or a forced pastoral termination can result.

The Program Church: 150 to 350 Members

The Program Church grows out of the necessity for a high-quality personal relationship with the pastor to be supplemented by other avenues
of spiritual feeding. Programs must now begin to fill that role.

The well-functioning Program Church has many cells of activity, which are headed up by lay leaders. These lay leaders, in addition to providing structure and guidance for these cells, also take on some pastoral functions. The Stewardship Committee gathers for its monthly meeting and the committee chair asks about a missing member. Upon being told that Mary Steward's daughter had to be taken to the hospital for an emergency operation, the chair will allow time for expressions of concern for Mary and her daughter. The chair may include both of them in a opening prayer. If the teacher of an adult class notices that someone in the class is feeling depressed, the teacher will often take the class member aside and inquire about his well-being. Even if the teacher eventually asks the pastor to intervene, the pastor has already gotten a lot of assistance from this lay leader.

Clergy are still at the center of the Program Church, but their role has shifted dramatically. Much of their time and attention must be spend in planning with other lay leaders to ensure the highest quality programs. The pastor must spend a lot of time recruiting people to head up these smaller ministries, training, supervising, and evaluating them, and seeing to it that their morale remains high. In essence the pastor must often step back from direct ministry with people to coordinate and support volunteers who offer this ministry. Unless the pastor gives high priority to the spiritual and pastoral needs of lay leaders, those programs will suffer.

To be sure, a member can expect a hospital or home call from the pastor when personal crisis or illness strikes. But members had better not expect this pastor to have a lot of time to drink coffee in people's kitchens. To see the pastor about a parish matter, they will probably have to make an appointment at the church office several weeks in advance.

When clergy move from a Pastoral Church to a Program Church, unless they are ready to shift from a primarily interpersonal mode to a program planning and development mode, they will experience tension and difficulty in their new congregation. It is not that clergy will have no further need for their interpersonal skills. Far from it—they need to depend on them even more. But now those interpersonal skills will be placed at the service of the parish program.

Key skills for effective ministry in a Program Church begin with the ability to pull together the diverse elements of the parish into a mission statement. Helping the parish arrive at a consensus about its direction is essential. Next the pastor must be able to lead the parish toward attaining the goals that arise out of that consensus. To wilt in the face of opposition to this consensus will be seen as a lack of leadership ability. The Program Church pastor will also need to be able to motivate the most capable lay persons in the parish to take on key components of the parish vision and help make it become a reality. Developing the trust and loyalty of these parish leaders and ensuring their continued spiritual growth and development is another key part of the cluster of skills needed in the Program Church.

For clergy who get their primary kicks out of direct pastoral care work, ministry in a Program Church may leave them with a chronic feeling of flatness and lack of fulfillment. Unless these clergy can learn to derive satisfaction from the work of pastoral administration, they should think twice about accepting a call to this size parish.

The Corporate Church: 350 or More Active Members

The quality of Sunday morning worship is the first thing you usually notice in a Corporate Church. Because these churches usually have abundant resources, they will usually have the finest organ and one of the best choirs in town. A lot of work goes into making Sunday worship a rich experience. The head of staff usually spends more time than other clergy preparing for preaching and worship leadership.

In very large Corporate Churches the head of staff may not even remember the names of many parishioners. When members are in the hospital it is almost taken for granted that they will be visited by an associate or assistant pastor, rather than the senior pastor. Those who value highly the Corporate Church experience are willing to sacrifice a personal connection with the senior pastor in favor of the Corporate Church's variety and quality of program offerings.

Sometimes the head pastor is so prominent that the personage of the pastor acquires a legendary quality, especially in the course of a long pastorate. Few may know this person well, but the role does not require it. The head pastor becomes a symbol of unity and stability in a very complicated congregational life.

The Corporate Church is distinguished from the Program Church by its complexity and diversity. The patriarchs and matriarchs return, but now as the governing boards who formally, not just informally, control the church's life and future. Laity lead on many levels, and the Corporate Church provides opportunity to move up the ladder of influence.

Key to the success of the Corporate Church is the multiple staff and its ability to manage the diversity of its ministries in a collegial manner. Maintaining energy and momentum in a Corporate Church is very difficult when there is division within the parish staff. Any inability to work together harmoniously is especially evident during Sunday worship where any tensions among the ordained leadership of the parish will manifest themselves in subtle ways.

It is at this point that clergy making the transition to the Corporate Church find themselves most vulnerable and unsupported. Our denominational systems do little to equip clergy to work collegially within a multiple staff. A three-day workshop on the multiple staff is a bare introduction. Leaders in industry with master's degrees in personnel management still make serious mistakes in hiring and developing leaders for the corporation. The head of staff of a Corporate Church learns to manage a multiple staff by trial and error. Sacrificing a few associate and assistant clergy on the altar of experience is the price the church pays for such lack of training.

For the most part clergy are not taught to work collegially. In seminary we compete with one another for grades. Each of us retreats to his or her own cubicle to write term papers. There is little interaction in class. In seminary we don't really have to take each other seriously. This might change if, for example, a professor were to assign four seminarians to complete research on a church doctrine, write one paper, and receive a group grade. In that kind of learning atmosphere we would have to take one another on and argue about our different theological perspectives and forms of piety. Unless our training can begin to equip us for collegial ministry, our seminaries will continue to turn out lone rangers who don't really have to work with other clergy until they get to the Corporate Church or the larger Program Church. By that time our patterns have been set.

The clergy who are called as head of staff in Corporate Churches are usually multi-skilled people who have proven their skill in a great variety of pastoral situations. In a multiple staff, however, the senior minister will need to delegate some of those pastoral tasks to other full-time staff members, who will inevitably want to do them differently.

Learning to allow these people to do things their own way is in itself a major new demand.

Our research with the Myers-Briggs Type Indicator shows that congregations are best served when the multiple staff includes different types. The more diverse the staff, the greater its ability to minister to a diverse congregation. But this requirement for diversity makes multiple staff functioning more complicated: The more diverse the staff, the harder it is to understand and support one another's ministries.

Lay leaders are generally completely baffled by the inability of ordained people to work collegially. "If our religious leaders aren't able to get along, what hope is there for this world?" they may wonder. Lay leaders could help enormously by seeing to it that there is money in the budget for regular consultative help for the staff. This help is not needed only when tensions arise. Multiple staffs need to be meeting regularly with an outside consultant to keep lines of communication open and difficulties surfaced.

When the multiple staff is having fun working well together, this graceful colleagueship becomes contagious throughout the Corporate Church. Lay people want to get on board and enjoy the camaraderie. The parish has little difficulty filling the many volunteer jobs needed to run a Corporate Church.

In addition to learning to manage a multiple staff, clergy making the transition to head of staff need to hone their administrative skills. These clergy are becoming chief executive officers of substantive operations. Yet I would emphasize leadership skills over management skills. While managers can manage the energy of a parish, leaders can *generate* energy. The Corporate Church needs leaders who know how to build momentum. Otherwise, even when managed well, these large churches run out of gas and begin to decline.

In summary, the most difficult transitions in size are from Pastoral to Program or, when downsizing, from Program to Pastoral. These are two very different ways to be church. More is required than a theoretical vision of the shift. We need to deal with the fact that a shift in size at this level just doesn't feel right to people. Somewhere deep inside they begin to sense that it doesn't feel like church anymore.

Choice Points for Clergy

It is not uncommon for parishioners to want to add a hundred new members to the parish but be unwilling to change one thing about their parish to accommodate the increase. We often refer to this as the vampire theory of growth: "We need some new blood around here." Basically members desire a bunch of new people to help pay the bills and to fill up the choir, Sunday school, and sanctuary, but they don't expect to make any sacrifices related to the things they want from their church.

Some of the greatest upheaval caused by numerical growth occurs when a congregation is on the borderline between two of the four different sizes of congregations described earlier. When a parish crosses the boundary between one size and another, it needs to begin relating to its clergy in fairly radically different ways than previously. As a review of these descriptions in a group setting, ask four participants to volunteer, each to summarize the dynamics of one of the four types of congregations. At the end of each summary ask the group if it remembers any additional points. Fill in any important aspects not brought up. Briefly discuss what description best suits your parish.

Remind the group that the most difficult transitions are between the Pastoral and Program Churches. The following activity will help illustrate what a transition from one size church to the other might mean.

Ask participants to stand and push the chairs to the side of the room, clearing the floor.

Rather than have participants simply circle answers to prepared questions, I like to send the "A's" to one side of the room and the "B's" to the other side. You can see at a glance where everyone stands on an issue, and the two groups can talk to each other about their choices. Since the questions deal with choices clergy need to make between two competing activities, I ask any clergy present to remain silent until the other participants have answered.

Have one side of the room represent response A and the other side represent response B. Read aloud one set of A-B choices. Have participants choose their responses by going to the designated side of the room. Tally the results. Allow up to two minutes for the two groups to discuss their stance, then go on to the next question.

Each set of questions represents a choice point for your pastor. Should your pastor have had a week full of crises and only limited time left, which response represents your preference for what the pastor should do?

A. Visit more shut-ins?
B. Prepare a better sermon?

A. Attend a wedding reception?
B. Go on a retreat with parish staff?

A. Call on prospective members?
B. Conduct a training session for church officers?

A. Visit a bereaved family?
B. Help two church officers resolve a conflict?

A. Make a hospital call on a fringe member?
B. Attend a continuing education event?

A. Give pastoral counseling to members?
B. Attend a planning event with officers?

A. Call on parishioners?
B. Recruit leaders for parish events?

A. Attend an activity with parish youth?
B. Critique a meeting with a church officer?

Once you have completed the exercise as a class, invite the pastor to share personal responses to each question. I encourage clergy to choose the activity they would most enjoy rather than the one they believe might claim a higher parish priority. The differences between the pastoral and lay responses to these questions may result in some fruitful discussion related to size of congregation and pastoral expectations.

This activity can point out several issues:

1. Congregations may be Program size yet still require their clergy to attend to all the category A pastoral activities. This is a perfect prescription for burnout. It can also lead to labeling clergy as "bad"

because they don't accomplish all the tasks in the A column while they are also expected to crank out quality programs for the parish (Category B activities).

2. Clergy in small Pastoral Churches should be focusing their energies and attention on the A activities. But sometimes because their background or training is in Program Churches, they continue to concentrate on the B activities or feel guilty because they aren't doing so.

3. Clergy and laity often disagree on priorities for clergy. This exercise often surfaces those differences quickly and makes role negotiation possible.

Staffing for Growth

Some congregations do not grow because they are not staffed for growth. If, for example, you are a Program Church, expecting your pastor to assist you in developing and executing quality programs in the church, yet you also expect your pastor to do pastoral calling in homes, you probably have a pastor who is doing neither task well and is burning out trying to do it all. Unless those pastoral expectations change or you add more staff, the congregation will not grow, as members are going to be dissatisfied with both the programs that are offered and the fact that they are not receiving the pastoral care they desire.

As a rule of thumb, if you desire to staff for growth, you need one full-time program person on your staff for every one hundred active members. (This does not include support staff such as janitors or secretaries.) *Active members* refers to how many are attending worship on the average year around. You are staffing for maintenance if you are just slightly under that figure. You are staffed for decline if you are seriously under that figure.

Growing churches see that their members as well as their visitors receive adequate pastoral care during times of crisis or need. People well cared for pastorally are inclined to invite their friends and family members to become affiliated with their parish. When a new family to your area is having difficulty, having a staff member make a call to discover ways the parish can meet needs makes a deep impression. Without that call, they are less likely to think of joining your congregation.

The addition of a paid professional, i.e., youth worker, religious education specialist, business manager, usually pays for itself within twelve to eighteen months. For example, a congregation with 225 active members that hires a third full-time staff member to provide better quality ministry will most likely to grow to 300 members.

Demographic Profiles: How Do Congregations Get Their Money's Worth?

By Alice Mann

Originally published in Congregations: The Alban Journal, *July/August 1995, 16-19. Demographic profiles described in this article are available from* Percept. *Call 1-800-442-6277.*

As I work with congregations on issues of growth and evangelization, I find that many churches have invested in a commercially prepared demographic profile of their ministry area—usually through a diocesan "package" program. What a gold mine! Not only are leaders spared the tedium of prying out by hand the proper census data for their ministry area; this basic material is now enhanced with a close analysis of local "lifestyle" subgroups and is summarized in an attractive graphic format.

So what happens to this valuable raw material? Some congregations can't get it because their judicatories have not "bought in" to the information service. (Your judicatory may have other sensible priorities at the moment, but this investment should at least be explored by relevant judicatory leaders.) Other congregations are hesitant to expend the modest fee for their individual profile. If they are concerned about growth —or about holding their own in a declining or shifting population—this attitude is "penny wise, pound foolish." But even when clergy and lay boards make this wise investment, they frequently don't get their full return. When I ask such leaders what they did with the material, the answer is almost always: "We looked it over when it came, but now it's in a drawer somewhere...."

If any of these scenarios sound familiar—if you've got a profile collecting dust somewhere, or if you have been wondering whether to purchase such information for your judicatory or congregation—here are some thoughts about how to "work" a demographic profile with a group of church leaders, so that this carload of "ore" gets converted into the real "gold" of mission clarity and creativity.

1. Set the Theological Context: It takes work to introduce marketing data to congregational leaders without allowing the whole marketing mentality to take over congregational thinking about growth. There is plenty of useful information in the "lifestyle" categories marketers have developed—in the poignant descriptions, for example, of "young blue-collar families" or "established empty-nesters." But we'd better keep in mind that market researchers who created these labels are finally interested in where people spend their money. We may well recall Jesus' observation, "Where your treasure is, there will your heart be also." But we don't want to substitute "consumer" for "child of God" as the core definition of a human being; nor do we want to adopt a shrunken definition of evangelization as "selling services of a religious nature."

It is the job of congregational leaders to find and use appropriate theological language about the task of evangelization. Happily, our national and regional church bodies have done a great deal of the groundwork. When I work with Episcopal congregations and their leaders, I usually explore with them—phase by phase—the definition formally adopted by our General Convention: "The presentation of Jesus Christ, in the power of the Holy Spirit, in such ways that people may be led to believe in him as Savior and follow him as Lord within the fellowship of the church." When a church is preparing to look at its demographic profile, it is important for leaders to return to **the theological statements, definitions, and sources** that have been helpful to them in the past—or to find some now—so that they are grounded in communal authority to interpret the facts *theologically*.

2. Establish a Climate of Contemplation: In contemplation, we lay aside the "action mode"—even our prayers of petition and intercession—in order to gaze quietly upon the face of the Other, the face of God. Such a clear-hearted gaze requires that we remain still in the presence of our inner distraction and drivenness, that we discover for ourselves the pathways of grace that may take us beyond anxiety or achievement—to a simpler "abiding" in God's love. Many congregations have little tradition of corporate contemplation. Their tolerance for communal silence is low, and they have few effective rituals of transition into a more reflective and receptive mode of being together.

Still, the congregation's "corporate spirituality" will be especially important as leaders consider the demographic report because this document profiles the "face of the other"—the most immediate neighbor in whom we are called to seek and serve Christ. Contemplative practices can't be imposed suddenly on an unprepared congregation without doing spiritual violence and provoking resistance. But leaders can consider what styles of reflective listening, what Bible stories and hymns, what special forms of prayer might be employed in preparation for, and in response to, presentation of the demographic profile. Most of all, the report should be introduced as part of an ongoing act of contemplation, the continuing expectations that the face of the stranger may reveal to us (as it did to Sarah and Abraham, or to Mary Magdalene at the tomb) the presence and promise of God.

3. Name the Congregation's Current Gifts and Vulnerabilities: The profile is complex and may seem a little overwhelming to discuss. One way to "ground" the conversation is to start with what God is already doing in the life of this congregation. Ask people to identify the special **gifts and strengths** of this church for which they give thanks. Then ask them to identify the congregation's **weaknesses and vulnerabilities**— areas in which the congregation especially needs God's help and guidance. Allow people time to list their responses individually, then collect the items in each category on a chart-pad, going round and round the group until every response on everyone's list is recorded without debate.

4. Look Together at the Broadest Information in the Demographic Profile: The first part of this discussion should focus on the question, **"Is our community's population growing, shrinking, or stable?"** This is easy to pick out from a chart of the census figures for population and households. Compare these trends with a chart showing average Sunday attendance over the same time span as the population graph. (Average all Sunday services that don't overlap in attendance, for all fifty-two Sundays of each relevant year).

With this data in view the group can consider a second key question: **"To what extent does our attendance history reflect population trends in the community?"** Don't skip to discussion of "why" without getting a clear consensus on the factual comparison between the figures: overall, is the attendance trend better, worse, or about the same when compared with the population trend? This is part of the act of contemplation—to allow the facts to register clearly in our awareness before running off to explain them or change them.

Once the numerical trends have been addressed, the group can consider graphs that chart household incomes, racial/ethnic proportions, and age distribution. After clarification, the leader might put a six-point scale on the board and pose the question: "To what extent does the congregation seem to match the community?" Ask people to do the rating individually and collect their scores on the chart before discussion proceeds. Otherwise, the complexities of interpretation can prevent people from making common sense observations. The leader can focus discussion by asking people to identify the main similarities and differences they observed; record these without insisting on consensus.

5. Look Together at the Top "Lifestyle" Groupings: Because marketers have created dozens of possible lifestyle categories to consider, and because the description of each category may include several pages of material, coherent group discussion is a real challenge. I would suggest that two members of the group meet ahead of time with the congregation's one-page profile summary and the accompanying lifestyle descriptions in hand. Start by making a large version of the **bar chart** showing the top five to seven lifestyle groups in the community and their percentages. Next, create one legible piece of newsprint to summarize the **characteristics of each key segment**. You will have to make some choices. If the description starts with a summary paragraph, look there first for phrases to list. If there is still space, draw from sections on religious affiliations and primary concerns, including percentage numbers if available. Remember that the profilers highlight characteristics that exceed the national average for that behavior; the fact that the group is more likely to read the Wall Street Journal than other groups doesn't necessarily mean that most of them read it. That's why it helps to list the actual percentages.

Begin the discussion period with biblical meditation, quiet, and prayer which calls the group **to contemplate the "face of the other."** Ask for "eyes to see" clearly those around us and "ears to hear" what God might say to us about how we are connected to these others. Having set the tone, ask people to look together at the bar chart of major groupings. Invite them to walk around the room to look at the sheets that describe each particular group. When the group reassembles, record the **"surprises"** people experienced as they looked on the face of their community. Look at the rating scale again—would anyone shift their rating of the "match"? Ask people to add new items to the lists of **similarities and differences** between community and congregation. As you conclude this piece of work, give people time to ask themselves what God might be saying to them about this information, and to share that with the group in some prayerful context.

The next step with the lifestyle segments makes use of your initial listing of the congregation's strengths and weaknesses. Hang those sheets up front again. Beside them, hang just two or three of the top lifestyle group descriptions—you'll probably want to start with the largest groups. Ask people to ponder the possible connections between the congregation's identity and that of the community. The leader should use two blank sheets to record responses—one marked **"Opportunities"** (for areas where church strengths might match community needs) and the other marked **"Threats"** (for community realities which seem like bad news for this congregation, given who we are right now).

Depending on the amount of time available and the energy available for this task, the group might do another "round" of the previous exercise, using two or three more of the top lifestyle segments. In my experience, congregations are not very familiar with this kind of exploration, and leaders may find it very tiring. No matter how many segments the group examines for "opportunities and threats," it is important to take one more step, so that the energies of parish leaders do not become dispersed across too many worries and too many possibilities.

6. Identify Critical Issues: Clear the board of everything except the sheets with strengths, weaknesses, opportunities, and threats. Clean up any obvious duplication among the entries. Count the total number of items on all four lists combined and number them on the charts. Let's say there are thirty-six entries in all. Divide that number by three to determine the number of votes each person will receive—in this example, each would get twelve "picks." Ask each person to note for themselves which twelve items are most important **for leaders to pay attention to in the coming year.** It doesn't matter which part of the list the items come from—one person may choose mostly strengths to focus on, while another may zero in on environmental threats. When all have chosen their items, members go to the board and put one check mark next to each issue they identified.

These choices form the basis of a list of **critical issues.** Usually about a third of the items will surface in the rating as clearly more important than the others. Look for the natural break points in the data— see if there are two to four "top issues," then another group of "important" ones before the numbers start to fall off more sharply. Get the group's endorsement of the "break points"; if someone notices an issue that didn't get a high rating but (in their mind) should, ask the group if they are comfortable adding it back in. (This is a moment when individual discernment may influence and deepen the group selection of issues.)

Transfer the items that surfaced as "critical issues" to a clean sheet, beginning with the highest rated item. Draw a line at the "break point" between the "top few" and the other "important" items; this will help clergy, lay boards, and task groups to focus their attention on those matters which the group identified as central. Finally decide how these issues will be pursued. To begin with, each of the "top few" should be explored further by some person or group and assigned **time on the agenda** of key decision-makers.

7. Follow Up: As the demographic information and the list of critical issues are shared with others in the congregation, be sure to start over again with the theological basis and the climate of contemplation. Rather than defending the list, offer it as the beginning of new conversion and discernment, with widening circles of participation. Verify your emerging perceptions with other information—such as interviews with your newest members and a contemplative walk (or drive) around your whole ministry area. Identify the simple next steps you can take to explore or implement proposals that have surfaced. Then do them. God will let you know if you're on the wrong track!

Chapter 1

1. Kenneth Blanchard is cited by Alan C. Klaas in the book *In Search of the Unchurched: Why People Don't Join Your Congregation* (Bethesda, Md.: The Alban Institute, 1996), p. 71. Blanchard's talk, "Personal Excellence in the 21st Century," is available on cassette from Convention Cassettes Unlimited (800-776-5454). The talk was delivered in 1994 to the Leadership Network of Dallas, Texas.

2. Lyle Schaller, Douglas Walrath, Carl Dudley, Carl George, Kennan Callahan, and Nancy Foltz are some of the writers who have described size differences.

3. Arlin Rothauge, *Sizing Up a Congregation for New Member Ministry* (New York: Episcopal Church Center, undated). Available from Episcopal Parish Services, 800-903-5544.

4. See two books by Carl F. George: *How to Break Growth Barriers* (Grand Rapids, Mich.: Baker Books, 1993), and *Prepare Your Church for the Future* (Grand Rapids, Mich.: Fleming H. Revell, 1992).

5. Stewart C. Zabriskie, *Total Ministry: Reclaiming the Ministry of All God's People* (Bethesda, Md.: The Alban Institute, 1995).

6. Alan C. Klaas, *Church Membership Initiative: Narrative Summary of Findings, Research Summary of Findings* (Appleton, Wis.: Aid Association for Lutherans, 1993).

7. Loren Mead, *Financial Meltdown in the Mainline?* (Bethesda, Md.: The Alban Institute, 1998).

Chapter 2

1. Charles Arn says that the current comfort zone is 30 to 36 inches. See chapter 6 for more on worship and a full citation of his article.

2. Adding minor or chapel-type services won't usually help with a growth plateau because the schedule and style of these services tend to appeal to a small subset of potential worshippers, and clergy cannot endlessly increase the number of weekend services they lead. An exception may occur at the family-to-pastoral size transition in more liturgical churches where an additional early service may help establish a multicell identity for the congregation and provide space for a more introverted spirituality.

3. Carl F. George, *Prepare Your Church for the Future* (Grand Rapids, Mich.: Fleming H. Revell, 1992), p. 45. All subsequent percentages offered in this section come from Carl George's summary.

4. In some denominations attendance is not reported at the end of the year as a fifty-two Sunday average, but as a selection of one or more "key Sundays." Congregations may have these reports at hand but not the worship record books from which the information was drawn. In that case, I would take the average of the key Sundays, perhaps eliminating Easter. As long as the same weeks are counted each year, such figures will at least give an index of the trends and changes. In the Episcopal Church (USA), the average of the three key Sundays, other than Easter, tends to be higher than the actual year-round attendance average. Churches in resort areas with dramatic seasonal population changes may need to plot their two seasons separately, because different factors may affect attendance during these two parts of the year. Most other churches see some summer decrease (exacerbated, I believe, by reduction in the number of worship services), but should simply include this seasonal variation in the year-round average.

Chapter 3

1. Those with an average attendance below 800.

2. There are exceptions to this observation. When a part-time pastor stays longer than a decade or so, or when endowment income has made it possible to retain a full-time pastor over the years, the dynamics of a family size church come to resemble, in many ways, those of a pastoral size church.

3. Speed B. Leas and George D. Parsons, *Understanding Your Congregation as a System* (Washington, D.C.: The Alban Institute, 1993), p. 126.

Chapter 4

1. An opening prayer at the Holy Eucharist in the *Book of Common Prayer* (New York: Church Hymnal Corporation, 1977).

2. A phrase I borrow, with great appreciation, from Celia Allison Hahn.

3. See the discussion of vigils and fasting in *Discerning Your Congregation's Future* by Roy Oswald and Bob Friedrich (Bethesda, Md.: The Alban Institute, 1996), introduction and appendix A.

4. Linda Clark, *Music in Churches: Nourishing Your Congregation's Musical Life* (Bethesda, Md.: The Alban Institute, 1994).

5. A new educational resource will soon be available based on Linda Clark's more recent work. It will include a video to illustrate style differences in congregations. Questions about publication can be directed to Dr. Clark at the School of Theology, Boston University.

6. See Charles M. Olsen's and Danny E. Morris's fine book *Discerning God's Will Together: A Spiritual Practice for the Church* (Bethesda, Md.: The Alban Institute, 1997).

Chapter 5

1. The work of Danny Miller and Peter Friesen *(Organizations: A Quantum View)* suggests the value of early resistance to a change in basic organizational configuration; this parallels John Kotter's notion about developing an adequate sense of urgency (*Leading Change*), and Ronald Heifetz's concept of allowing issues to "ripen" (*Leadership Without Easy Answers*). These issues are discussed more extensively in chapter 8.

2. Lyle E. Schaller, *44 Questions for Church Planters*, (Nashville: Abingdon Press, 1991), chapter 1.

3. Christian Schwarz, *Natural Church Development* (Carol Stream, Ill.: ChurchSmart Resources, 1996). This organization can be reached at 800-253-4276.

4. Alan C. Klaas, *Church Membership Initiative: Narrative Summary of Findings, Research Summary of Findings* (Appleton, Wis.: Aid Association for Lutherans, 1993).

5. This is my own observation, not a finding of the Church Membership Initiative study.

6. Schwarz, *Natural Church Development*, p. 110.

7. The *Church Membership Initiative* estimated that 60 percent of

the overall growth or decline of churches over time can be attributed to factors in the local community or wider environment over which the church has no control–so-called "contextual" factors.

Chapter 6

1. Charles, Arn. "Multiple Worship Services and Church Growth," *Journal of the American Society of Church Growth* 7 (1996): 73.

2. Ibid. Arn says that seating-capacity estimates must be updated with cultural change. A pew that was estimated to seat five people a generation ago would now comfortably seat only three because the comfort zone has grown to 30 to 36 inches.

3. Ibid., p 88.

4. Ibid., p. 94. Arn is citing a study by the Church of the Nazarene.

5. Ibid.

6. Ibid., p. 95.

7. See Roy Oswald's book *Clergy Self-Care: Finding a Balance for Effective Ministry* (Washington, D.C.: The Alban Institute, 1991).

8. Arn, "Multiple Worship Services and Church Growth," pp. 103-4.

9. Ibid., p. 101.

Chapter 7

1. Carl F. George, *How to Break Growth Barriers: Capturing Overlooked Opportunities for Church Growth* (Grand Rapids, Mich.: Baker Books, 1993), p. 158.

2. Bill Sullivan, *Ten Steps to Breaking the 200 Barrier* (Kansas City, Mo.: Beacon Hill Press, 1988), p. 51.

Chapter 8

1. Ronald A. Heifetz, *Leadership Without Easy Answers* (Cambridge, Mass.: The Belknap Press, 1994), chapter 4.

2. Roy Oswald, *Making Your Church More Inviting* (Washington, D.C.: The Alban Institute, 1992), chapter 6.

3. Heifetz, *Leadership Without Easy Answers*, p. 128.

4. John Kotter, "Leading Change: Why Transformation Efforts Fail," *Harvard Business Review* (March-April 1995): 61.

5. Ibid., p. 62.

6. Peter Friesen and Danny Miller, *Organizations: A Quantum View* (Englewood Cliffs, N.J.: Prentice-Hall, 1984), p. 225.

7. Ibid.

8. C. Kirk Hadaway and David A. Roozen, *Rerouting the Protestant Mainstream: Sources of Growth & Opportunities for Change* (Nashville: Abingdon Press, 1995). Cited from "Spiritual Revival on the Mainline," an excerpt of the book which appeared in *The Christian Ministry* (January-February 1995): 25-27.

9. Kotter, "Leading Change," p. 62.

10. Ibid., p. 60.

11. Ibid.

12. Gilbert R. Rendle, "On Not Fixing the Church," *Congregations: The Alban Journal* (May-June 1997): 15.

13. Ibid., p. 16.

14. This is an adaptation of Carl George's "Berry Bucket Theory," which he presented in *How to Break Church Growth Barriers* (Grand Rapids, Mich.: Baker Books, 1993), p. 112.

15. See *The Inviting Church* by Roy Oswald and Speed B. Leas, and *Making Your Church More Inviting* by Roy Oswald. The latter volume, a workbook, provides a detailed process for gathering information from visitors and newcomers to your church.

16. Kotter, "Leading Change," p. 63.

17. See note 15 above for resources.

18. See Christian Schwarz's comments on multiplication of ministries in *Natural Church Development* (Carol Stream, Ill.: ChurchSmart Resources, 1996), part 3.

19. These suggestions about making the change quickly come from Bill Sullivan, *Ten Steps to Breaking the 200 Barrier* (Kansas City, Mo.: Beacon Hill Press, 1988), chapters 4 and 8.

BIBLIOGRAPHY

Arn, Charles. *How to Start a New Service*. Grand Rapids, Mich.: Baker Books, 1997.

_____. "Multiple Worship Services and Church Growth." *Journal of the American Society of Church Growth* 7 (1996): 73-104.

Blanchard, Kenneth. "Personal Excellence in the 21st Century," a talk delivered in 1994 to the Leadership Network of Dallas, Texas. Available on cassette from Convention Cassettes Unlimited (800-776-5454).

Book of Common Prayer. New York: Church Hymnal Corporation, 1977.

Clark, Linda. *Music in Churches: Nourishing Your Congregation's Musical Life*. Bethesda, Md.: the Alban Institute, 1994.

Friedrich, Bob, and Roy Oswald. *Discerning Your Congregation's Future*. Bethesda, Md.: the Alban Institute, 1996.

Friesen, Peter, and Danny Miller. *Organizations: A Quantum View*. Englewood Cliffs, N.J.: Prentice Hall, 1984.

George, Carl F. *How to Break Growth Barriers*. Grand Rapids, Mich.: Baker Books, 1993.

_____. *Prepare Your Church for the Future*. Grand Rapids, Mich.: Fleming H. Revell Co., 1992.

Hadaway, C. Kirk, and David A. Roozen. "Spiritual Revival on the Mainline," an excerpt from the book *Rerouting the Protestant Mainstream: Sources of Growth and Opportunities for Change.* (Nashville: Abingdon Press, 1995), *The Christian Ministry* (January-February 1995): 25-27.

Heifetz, Ronald A. *Leadership Without Easy Answers.* Cambridge, Mass.: The Belknap Press, 1994.

Klaas, Alan C. *In Search of the Unchurched: Why People Don't Join Your Congregation.* Bethesda, Md.: the Alban Institute, 1996.

_____. Church Membership Initiative. *Narrative Summary of Findings, Research Summary of Findings.* Appleton, Wis.: Aid Association for Lutherans, 1993.

Kotter, John. "Leading Change: Why Transformation Efforts Fail." *Harvard Business Review* (March-April 1995): 59-67.

Leas, Speed B., and Roy M. Oswald. *The Inviting Church.* 1987. Reprint. Washington, D.C.: the Alban Institute, 1993

Leas, Speed B., and George D. Parsons. *Understanding Your Congregation As a System.* Washington, D.C.: the Alban Institute, 1993.

Mead, Loren. *Financial Meltdown in the Mainline?* Bethesda, Md.: the Alban Institute, 1998.

Morris, Danny E., and Charles M. Olsen. *Discerning God's Will Together: A Spiritual Practice for the Church.* Bethesda, Md.: the Alban Institute, 1997.

Oswald, Roy M. *Clergy Self-Care: Finding a Balance for Effective Ministry.* Washington, D.C.: the Alban Institute, 1991.

_____. *Making Your Church More Inviting.* Washington, D.C.: the Alban Institute, 1992.

Rendle, Gilbert R. "On Not Fixing the Church." *Congregations: The Alban Journal* (May-June 1997): 15-17.

Rothauge, Arlin. *Sizing Up a Congregation for New Member Ministry.* New York: Episcopal Church Center (undated). Available from Episcopal Parish Services, 800-903-5544.

Schaller, Lyle E. *44 Questions for Church Planters.* Nashville: Abingdon Press, 1991.

Schwarz, Christian. *Natural Church Development.* Carol Stream, Ill.: ChurchSmart Resources, 1994.

Sullivan, Bill. *Ten Steps to Breaking the 200 Barrier.* Kansas City, Mo.: Beacon Hill Press, 1988.

Zabriskie, Stewart C. *Total Ministry: Reclaiming the Ministry of All God's People.* Bethesda, Md.: the Alban Institute, 1995.